Emotional Intimacy 101:
The Surefire Way to Great Romantic Relationships

Pierre F. Steenberg, Ph.D., D.Min.

Designing Hearts
Publications

Editing: Dr. R. Meyer
Proofing: Steve Hix

All Rights Reserved. No part of this book may be reproduced, duplicated, reposted or transmitted in any form or by any means, electronically or mechanically, including photocopying, recording, or by any information storage and retrieval system, without the express written permission of the author and copyright owner. Any unauthorized copying, reproduction, translation, or distribution of any part of this material without express written permission of the author is prohibited and against the law.

Disclaimer and Terms of Use: No information contained in this book should be considered as a counseling or advising relationship between the author and the reader or anyone else. No information contained in this book should be considered as marital or relational advice. Your reliance upon and use of information and content of this book is solely at your own discretion and risk. The author assumes no liability of any nature or responsibility for damage to any relationship, or injury to you, other persons, or property arising from any use of any product, information, idea, or instruction contained in the content provided to you through this book.

Available from **Amazon.Com** and other retailers

DEDICATION

To my parents who were the most wonderful role models
of the perfect marriage.

CONTENTS

ACKNOWLEDGMENTS

This book is based on a doctoral thesis researching emotional intimacy. I am grateful and thankful to the professors who were part of this journey, who encouraged me, and who guided my steps. A great deal of credit also goes to the couples that participated in the research. They opened up their private lives and granted permission to use their insight, experience, and stories to assist others through research and publications such as this one.

A WORD ABOUT QUALITATIVE RESEARCH

People and their relationships are very complex. No two people are the same. This not only goes for biometrics, a statistical study of biological data, such as finger prints, DNA patterning, ear shapes, iris patterns (that is the colored part of the eye regulating the light entering the eye), voice patterns, and so forth, but also for our thinking, emotions, experiences, and the like.

There is no valid research, nor would there ever be any valid study regarding relationships, that stated that all people acted in a specific way, or had thoughts according to one definite method, or experienced something always in a particular way relationally. We are just too different.

That does not mean that there are no generalities between people, ringing true for most people. People are still people and share certain commonalities, such as desires. This book makes use of certain generalities, which may not be true for every reader at every point.

These generalities have been shown by way of academically sound research to be valid for many people. There will always be those for whom certain aspects differ. That does not in any way invalidate the research. The research only claims that something is the case for most people. Please apply the concept of the bell curve to illustrate the point further.

❧ CHAPTER ONE ☙

INTRODUCTION

What is love? It is suggested that true love has three elements: Emotional intimacy, physical passion, and commitment; (compare Sternberg, Robert J. 1988. The triangle of love: intimacy, passion, commitment. New York: Basic Books). May I be so bold to suggest that true love has one more element, namely, "relational safety"? In both true love and romantic love one of these four elements stands out, emotional intimacy. Emotional intimacy is the fabric romantic relationships consist of. When a relationship is based only on physical intimacy that relationship is hollow and empty. When it is based only on safety it is co-dependent. When it is based only on commitment it becomes co-habitation.

Physical attraction may be the spark that lights the fire of physical intimacy, but emotional intimacy is the fuel that keeps that fire going. Especially for women, emotional intimacy is required to sustain and intensify physical intimacy. More and deeper emotional intimacy is the surefire way to greater physical intimacy. Emotional intimacy supplies the relational aspect of the relationship:

- One can be physically intimate without having a relationship at all; it is called prostitution, an unfulfilled and meaningless relationship.

- Similarly, people can be in a safe and demanding relationship where, "I need you and you need me", without having a real deep, meaningful, and loving relationship; it is called a co-dependent relationship.
- People can be in relationships of commitment and co-habitation relationships without any romance; it is called a plutonic relationship.
- People can experience emotional intimacy, which is the vital component of relationships; it is called significant and meaning-ful romantic and loving relationships.

It is emotional intimacy that adds a true and healthy friendship to the relationship. It is emotional intimacy that adds depth to the relationship. What used to be great romantic relationships lose their luster over time when emotional intimacy declines. Emotional intimacy can and has to be created continuously if the relationship is to remain happy, healthy, fulfilling, and ongoing.

Men and women approach emotional intimacy from very different perspectives. In fact, there are important gender differences regarding emotional intimacy, which cause misinterpretations and failed attempts to enhance emotional intimacy. We may think that we know the opposite gender well enough to understand how their emotional intimacy functions, but in reality we are often not able to comprehend it. We often do not even fathom how emotional intimacy works.

Imagine walking in a forest, which is in a pristine and unspoiled location. The birds sing, the streams flow, and the leaves are green. It is a wonderful day, filled with happiness. The trail curves around rocks and trees. As you walk around the rocks, a ruthless, hungry grizzly bear looms large in front of you. The wonderful day filled with contentment is suddenly not so pleasing anymore, and it is crammed with panic.

The bear advances aggressively; your heart rate shoots up and a wet sweat starts covering you, while shallow, short breaths follow. You fear you won't be able to escape; the bear has become your enemy.

Now, imagine a bear walking in a forest. It is in a pristine and unspoiled location. The birds sing, the streams flow, and the leaves are green. It is a wonderful day, filled with happiness. The grizzly bear is hungry and searching for food. As the bear follows the trail around some rocks there in front of it is a delicious, well-sized, and an easy accessible meal; you. The bear's day has just changed from a wonderful day to a great day. The bear does not see an enemy, but a great opportunity to a wonderful meal.

If a person found himself or herself in this dilemma, it is only natural for the human mind to think of the situation from his or her own perspective of danger, fear, and panic. Similarly the bear does not think of this person as a scared human being struggling to survive, instead it is licking its lips in anticipation of a succulent meal. The bear is driven by hunger and unaware of the human perspective. It would not help to attempt persuading the bear to leave you alone because you love bears, that you campaign for the environment, that you support open and free bear habitats. This plea for freedom makes sense only from the human perspective and not from the bear's perspective. The bear is not capable of understanding the human perspective. If you wish to survive, it may make better sense to point the bear to an alternate food source, such as your lunch bag, because now you are addressing the issue from the bear's perspective, hunger, rather than your own framework which is fear.

Men and women also have very different perspectives on emotional intimacy. Attempting to enhance emotional intimacy between you two may best be approached from your partner's perspective. Your perspective may not make sense to him or her. Even if your perspective makes sense to him or her it would probably not address his or her needs. The bear was in need of food, and you were in need of survival. Pleading for survival, making the bear understand the importance of your survival, or any topic regarding your survival is rather irrelevant to the bear even if the bear would have been able to understand it. Similarly, the bear could explain to you how hungry it was after its hibernation, how delicious you appeared, and even promised to kill you pain-free; everything about the bear's need for food is irrelevant to your need for survival. Your need for survival and the bear's need for food blind both of you to the other's perspective. The only happy ending for both is a well-fed bear and a safe unharmed human being.

Our needs and perspectives are often directly opposed to each other. As human beings we can learn from each other's needs and perspectives. If we would become aware of our spouse's needs and perspectives it would help us to see the benefits of sacrificing our lunch (by giving it to the bear) to save and enrich the relationship.

At times we may not even know what enhances our own emotional intimacy with someone else. How then would I ascertain what would enrich the other person's emotional intimacy toward me? Recent research,* a doctoral dissertation by the author, and years of practicing pastoral marital counseling provided me with both the insights and inspiration to write Emotional Intimacy 101: The Surefire Way To Great Romantic Relationships. This research revealed that there are many gender differences concerning emotional intimacy. In the actual research more than one couple commented that just answering the questions taught them a great deal about emotional intimacy. Yes, we can learn to become more aware of these gender differences and we can learn to enrich emotional intimacy.

If you are a male, what would you think after years of marriage if your wife asked you to talk to her and then she kept quiet? Then, if you asked her what she would like to talk about she would say that she did not know. If you are a female, let me ask whether you have ever wondered why your husband had nothing to say to you, but when he was with visitors he would come up with all these interesting anecdotes? Have you wondered why he did not share them with you?

Wives, did you know that men linked empathy and support and viewed both of them very differently from how you view them? Different comprehension of emotional intimacy and personal needs between genders often lead to misfires of emotional intimacy. Understanding these crossed-gender differences and needs, and creating the appropriate changes to account for these differences and needs often leads to surefire growth in emotional intimacy. This would fire up your romantic relationship.

---

* All the stories used in the book were quoted with the permission of the couples who participated in the research. To protect their identities, however, all names will be pseudonyms. The couples were aware of, and assumed the risk of someone, perhaps a friend, recognizing their stories.

❧ CHAPTER TWO ❧

BIG BANG, LITTLE SPARK

A most important question is what is emotional intimacy, and what enhances it. Emotional intimacy will be defined and described in practical terms in chapter six entitled: "The Unexpected Gift to Emotional Intimacy." This chapter deals with the question "what enhances it?"

A recent doctoral research project, interviewed couples about emotional intimacy and what enhances it. The interviews lasted between an hour and two and a half hours each.

Two psychological theories were used to design the interview questions and to analyze the responses: The first was "Attachment Theory." This theory deals specifically with how attachment bonds are formed. Relational attachment bonding plays an important part in emotional intimacy. The second was "Narrative Theory." This theory was used to examine stories the couples told about successful and unsuccessful attempts to enrich emotional intimacy. This was useful to measure the impact or lack thereof of these attempts on the recipients.

The research questions were divided into various parts. One part used research questions to find out what people think enhances or diminishes emotional intimacy and how people actually try to improve and enrich emotional intimacy. Another part measured the efficacy or success of those attempts. The research provided us with a rare view of what improves emotional intimacy and what diminishes it.

Surprisingly, the research also revealed that the main impact on emotional intimacy did not come from a cognitive, rational or intellectual attempt at increasing emotional intimacy. Similarly, various efforts to enhance emotional intimacy were found to be ineffective. Lastly, it was discovered that gender differences made a major impact on emotional intimacy. These gender differences often worked against each other, resulting in a decline of emotional intimacy.

Couples were asked, "What do the words 'emotional intimacy' mean to you?" Both men and women coped well with characterizing or defining emotional intimacy, although women seemed to have a clearer understanding than men of what emotional intimacy was. It was the second question, however that was problematic, namely, "What increases emotional intimacy?"

It was interesting to note that women knew very clearly what they wished to happen with regard to enriching their emotional intimacy. Before emotional intimacy occurred, men, on the other hand, rarely knew what actually increased their own emotional intimacy, let alone knowing how to enhance their spouses' emotional intimacy. Just as women knew for certain what increased their emotional intimacy, men were certain what diminished theirs. As men did not really know what increased their wives' emotional intimacy, women similarly had no idea what diminished their husbands' emotional intimacy. The bottom line was that people seemed to be fairly oblivious about cross-gender emotional intimacy. No wonder so many romantic relationships fail.

Men seemed totally ignorant, at times, of how and why they made a negative impact on their spouses' emotional intimacy, and in some cases they were even unaware of having made any impact on their spouses' emotional intimacy. Men were able to identify whether emotional intimacy increased, or diminished, after it happened, but frequently they did not understand the mechanics behind enriching their spouses' emotional intimacy and what drained it. Similarly, women often had no idea that they weakened their husbands' emotional intimacy. Interestingly, women seemed to reduce their husbands' emotional intimacy while attempting to increase their own emotional intimacy. There was a disconnect between how the two genders understood emotional intimacy needs and the process of increasing or diminishing emotional intimacy.

The reason why men and women were not aware of these impacts on the others' emotional intimacy was because men and women's emotional intimacy needs often inversely affect the other one's intimacy. In other words, the very thing that enhanced her emotional intimacy might reduce his, and vice versa. Since the different genders did not know, how the other one's emotional intimacy worked, or that emotional intimacy works differently between the two genders, in general we assumed that the opposite gender's emotional intimacy works like ours, as we are the only ones aware of our own feelings if we do not make them known to others.

So when a woman asks a man to talk to her about what worries him, she thinks his emotional intimacy will grow towards her because her intimacy will certainly grow towards him. His emotional intimacy, however, does not work in the same way as hers. Sharing worries drains his emotional intimacy, and the more she asks him to share his worries the more it drains his emotional intimacy. The inverse is also true. The more he does not tell her what worries him the more her emotional intimacy gets drained. This topic will be explored in chapter seven, entitled, "To Know" Or "Not To Know?" If our emotional intimacy inversely affects each other, how then can both his and her emotional intimacy grow at the same time?

Perhaps cross-gendered emotional intimacy can best be explained by the way people express themselves in emotional terms. Let's say he conveys emotional intimacy in one specific way of communication, while she conveys it in another way of interaction. He tells her how close he feels to her and that he desires to feel even more attached to her. To facilitate his closer attachment he tells her what she could do to increase closeness to him.

There is a problem, however; she does not understand his communication or "language" of emotional intimacy, or the way he expresses it. She has no idea what he is saying; he is speaking in a foreign "language" to her. So, she starts to feel frustrated. She tells him that she feels lonely and isolated; although they are together, she lacks meaningful interaction and the sharing of feelings and thoughts. There is a another problem, however; he does not understand her way of conveying emotional intimacy, her expression or "language" of intimacy, and he also begins to feel frustrated with disastrous results; the more frustrated they feel the more they tell each other their own needs. This, however, makes no difference, as they do not "understand" each other's communication. So they think, "If we cannot use 'language' or conveying expressions of intimacy towards communicating emotional intimacy we will just demonstrate it by 'showing' each other." This new attempt, however, is also found to be ineffective as they soon realize that not only do they use different emotional intimacy expressions and "languages", they also use different ways of demonstrating emotional intimacy, or demonstration "languages." How can they comprehend, fathom and "understand" each other when each of them can only demonstrate and "speak" in one emotional "language", which happens to be different from the emotional "language" of the other? What makes sense for the one does not make sense to the other. What fulfills the one's emotional intimacy needs does not fulfill the other's.

Often couples just assume that they have the same needs and that emotional intimacy works in the same way for both spouses. They may be oblivious of the fact that these differences exist. If many of us are unaware of these differences how then can we comprehend and understand these differences between us? The coming chapters will attempt to explain male and female emotional intimacy needs and ways of expression or "languages."

Let's get back to the research. When asked what they did to enhance their spouses' emotional intimacy both genders stated that they assisted one another by performing favors. "Doing things" for each other was a conscious attempt to enrich the other person's emotional intimacy. With all couples and all genders reporting that "doing things" for each other was an attempt at increasing emotional intimacy between them, one would expect that it would actually work. When they "did things" for each other it was with the *"big bang"* expectation of making a *"big spark"* positive impact on the emotional intimacy between them. Later in the interview process the husbands were asked how what the wives did for them made an impact on their emotional intimacy towards their wives. The same question was also asked of the wives.

The answers to the questions and the narrative theory analysis of both genders' answers revealed that "doing things" for each other were nothing but a *"big bang"* with a *"little spark."* Both genders were of the opinion that "doing things" for each other would intensify their emotional intimacy, but no wife reported any increase in emotional intimacy because of these good deeds, nor did any husband. Both spouses said that they really appreciated this action and that it was very polite and kind of their spouses, but this did not intensify their emotional intimacy.

Similarly, both genders mentioned that they employed touch to increase emotional intimacy between them. Both genders stated confidently that touch would increase their spouses' emotional intimacy towards them. Touch, like "doing things" for one another, was believed to be *"big bang"* attempts to *"spark"* or incite emotional intimacy. Consequently, touch was frequently used by both genders with *"big bang"* expectations, but no *"sparks"* were reported. The men stated that they enjoyed touch, but no man reported an increase in emotional intimacy due to touch. For women touch fared even worse as a means of increasing emotional intimacy.

In other words, when an interviewee wanted to raise emotional intimacy they often "did things" for each other and used physical touch, but when asked what actually nurtured emotional intimacy no one mentioned "having things done" for them or physical touch. The interviews seem to support the minimalistic effect of "doing things" for each other and physical touch on emotional intimacy. Every time "doing things" for each other and physical touch was mentioned during the efficacy or effectiveness measurement part of the interviews, it was mentioned in passing without any discussion or a great deal of impact or influence.

"Doing things" for each other and touching each other are very important in any relationship, but in terms of nurturing emotional intimacy both over-promised and under-delivered. Touch may play a more prominent role in physical intimacy than emotional intimacy.

Since both genders mentioned "doing things" for each other and touching each other as tools or methods to increase emotional intimacy, and since both genders wished to stimulate emotional intimacy these two tools or methods were often used in the relationship, but the desired impact on emotional intimacy was small providing very little *"spark."*

It would be interesting to research whether the absence of "doing things" for each other or the lack of touch would harm emotional intimacy, but this question was not within the scope of this particular research. Years of counseling experience, however, suggest that the absence of both would be harmful. So, perhaps "doing things" for one another and touching each other are necessary in romantic relationships, and play a role in helping to maintain emotional intimacy rather than to stimulate it. Using them as a means of increasing emotional intimacy may carry *"big bang"* expectations yet yields little or no *"spark"* or incentive. These tools or methods, such as performing tasks and touching, are simply ineffective at stimulating emotional intimacy.

They are not bad tools, but they are just not suited to this task. Who would use a screwdriver to pound in a nail? Yet, we "do things" continuously for each other and touch one another as "tools" or means to stimulate emotional intimacy. When a screwdriver does not work well to drive a nail into a wall, however, it does not mean that we abandon screw drivers altogether. We need to learn to use hammers specifically for nails and screw drivers specifically for screws.

So, please feel free to continue to "do things" for each other as those actions have been reported as being highly appreciated. In addition, there is also a standing invitation to continue to touch each other. These actions were certainly not shown to diminish emotional intimacy. There may also be many other benefits added to these actions, unrelated to generating emotional intimacy; but please, do not have great expectations of stimulating emotional intimacy by these means. The resulting little *"spark"* or incentive will surely disappoint the *"big bang"* or immense expectation.

❧ CHAPTER THREE ☙

THE REAL BIG BANG WITH SUREFIRE SPARK

Remember when you were a toddler. One day you went with your parents to visit someone at his or her home. A vicious dog attacked you as you got out of the car and walked towards his or her house. Without even thinking you grabbed your parent's hand. You may also have clung onto your dad's leg for dear life.

Whenever we experience distress we seek closeness to other people. Seeking proximity is one of the classic signs of wanting attachment and bonding; in this case for protection. Children have many contact-seeking behaviors, for example, crying, lifting up both arms in an attempt to be picked up, moving closer to, making eye contact with, and so forth. In the case of the fierce dog dad responded to your "call" for help. That response could have taken the form of support, comfort or reassurance, or your distress could have been downplayed, or your frightened reactions could have been ignored. Every time you experienced anguish, for whatever reason, for real or perceived agony, and called for help either verbally or by means of body language and seeking proximity, a primary caregiver responded in one of the following three ways: Consistent support, inconsistent support, when you were supported some times, but when your need was downplayed at other times, or no support.

Whenever this happens the human mind embarks on calculating the measure of support or non-support. You ask, is my caregiver available and willing to meet my needs? A consistent affirmative answer shapes attachment to the caregiver positively with a Secure Attachment as result. An equivocal answer, indicating maybe, denoting sometimes "yes" and sometimes "no", shapes attachment negatively and leads to an Insecure Attachment. A negative answer, indicating "no", also shapes a bond negatively, bringing about an Insecure Attachment. As we grow up these experiences accumulate and before long we can see a pattern in the caregivers' reaction to our pleas for help.

Children who experienced a pattern of possibility, a "maybe" or perchance response from their caregivers often become preoccupied with, or anxious regarding attachment. Frequently there is no explanation why the parent or caregiver was supportive at times and not supportive at other times. These children tend to think, "If I only try harder, my parents will support me"; in other words, they reason, more effort to obtain support may lead to more support. People who are preoccupied with attachment typically do everything they can to become attached to others and to gain their support. These are the people whom others may regard as "high maintenance people." When you meet such a person on an airplane the conversation usually becomes "deep" or profound, and personal within minutes from that person's side. The person might hardly know you for five minutes, yet will tell you all about his or her troubled marriage, his or her struggling child, or a crisis that might be experienced. The person makes an effort to connect with you. After the airplane landed such a person might walk with you to the baggage claim department, continuing the conversation all the way. When departing, this person might greet you as a long lost friend and may even attempt to exchange contact information.

Children who experienced a consistent pattern of negative or "no" responses to their crises often avoided attachment permanently (unless a long and deep relationship with a securely attached person is formed). Attempts to obtain positive support responses did not materialize. Eventually such efforts were terminated; they did not work anyway, so, "why bother?" became a motto. These people are often seen and regarded as "loners"; they do their "own thing" and apparently do not need attachment or bonding. They are not inclined to discuss private and personal issues with others. Usually they do not consistently depend a great deal on others and they are not fond of others depending on them. They like to be left alone. This does not mean that they do not need support or that they do not experience distress. It simply means that they do not show it regularly. Experiments have continually demonstrated that they experience the same amount of distress internally when it is justified. "Loners" in a world of their own need more "space", while people "preoccupied" and driven by fixation need more bonding. People, who are securely connected, maintain a balance between the need for space and attachment. Their need for space and attachment seem less severe than the other two groups of people.

Consequently, as we grow up we adopt one of the following attachment styles: *Secure Attachment*, *Preoccupied Attachment*, called *"Ambivalent"* or *"Anxious" Attachment* in adults, and *Avoidant Attachment*, called *"Dismissive" Attachment* in adults. For our purposes here, and to avoid confusion, the terms "Preoccupied" and "Avoidant" will be used regardless of whether we are talking about children or adults. It should also be noted that there is a fourth attachment style called "Fearful" Attachment. Since this fourth attachment style is rare and usually involves mental health issues of the caregiver or the child it will not be dealt with here.

These attachment styles have a great impact on our emotional intimacy and adult relationships; for example, if two people who are preoccupied with attachment get married, they may cling obsessively to each other. Consequently, jealousy could become an issue between them. "Independence" or even "inter-dependence" may be shunned. If two people with an Avoidant Attachment pattern get married they might lead "separate" lives. Each spouse is then typically content to be "alone" and to do things single-handedly and unaccompanied. Consequently, they might get involved in different groups. They also enjoy each other, but become aware of and find more space between them than other couples.

If a person is preoccupied with attachment and gets married to a person who is avoidant that marriage often plays a "cat and mouse" game, or "catch me if you can" with attachment, or "a mouse runs circles around" dysfunctional attachment. The preoccupied person might seek more and deeper attachment, while the person avoiding attachment seeks more space. As the preoccupied person seeks additional attachment, the person avoiding bonding feels more smothered and pulls back even further. The more the "avoidant person" pulls back the more the "preoccupied person" feels alone and unattached. To resolve these feelings he or she seeks more attachment, trying more vigorously to obtain it. A negative downward spiral develops, frustrating both.

If two people who are emotionally securely attached get married, in general there seems to be a balance between emotional closeness and independence. They form a "team"; they depend on each other and have no problem if one spouse depends on the other. When they experience space between them they are not as far apart as one would expect an "avoidant person" to be from their partner. Securely attached relationships tend to be happier and more content than insecurely attached relationships. If a Securely Attached person marries a "Preoccupied" or an "Avoidant" person the "Preoccupied" and/or "Avoidant" person usually becomes Securely Attached over time, barring any abnormalities or dysfunctional behavior. Securely Attached people often find other Securely Attached people attractive, not referring to "physical" attraction but to "relational" attraction. Similarly, however, Insecurely Attached people mostly find other Insecurely Attached people attractive.

Our attachment styles make an impact on all our relationships with other people, whether married to them or not. They even have an influence on how we view others, generally speaking. How we view and regard others has an effect on how we relate to them, which in turn affects the relationship.

Securely Attached people typically have memories of warm and affectionate parents or caregivers. Others are often very fond of them while they think of others as generally well-intentioned and good-hearted. They view most people as being trustworthy and dependable.

People avoiding attachment typically have memories of "cold", unsympathetic and snubbing, cold-shouldering and rejecting mothers. They are often suspicious of other people's motives. They do not look at most people as trustworthy or dependable. "Avoidant people" tend to limit emotional intimacy to satisfy their own need for autonomy. They may place more emphasis on goals and achievement than on relationships and consequently, appear "driven" or ambitious, and successful in their work. This does not mean that their marriages are equally successful and fulfilling. People avoiding attachment may also withhold intimate disclosure.

People whose attachment style is preoccupied tend to remember their fathers as being unfair. They regard other people as complex and difficult to understand. They desire extreme emotional intimacy with anyone and everyone. These people are known to fear rejection. Others often misguidedly consider their fear of rejection with being too sensitive. When they complain, it is often done to gain acceptance and attachment rather than to draw attention to the topic they complained about.

These characteristics of the three attachment styles are credited to the following chapter: Feeney, Judith A. 1999. Adult Romantic Attachment and Couple Relationships. In, Handbook of Attachment Theory and Research. Eds. Cassidy, J, and Shaver, P R., 355-377. New York: Guilford Press.

To a large extent we can see how our attachment styles make an impact on relationships. We have also observed that emotional bonds, attachments between people, are on the whole determined by whether or not someone has been supported during a time of perceived or real danger, threat, and distress. It is evident that our attachment styles make an impact not only on our relationships, but also and especially on our emotional intimacy with other people. Being consistently supported in a time of crisis has a "big bang" or significant impact on our attachment and emotional intimacy. This is true for children as well as adults. With this psychological background regarding attachment formation and influence in mind, our attention turns to the substantial or "big bang" impact on emotional intimacy.

During the research regarding emotional intimacy mentioned earlier, every couple interviewed stated that the substantial or "big bang" impact, (the actual effect rather than an attempt to gain emotional intimacy) was a spouse's response to a crisis in their own lives. Except for one couple all the others mentioned a time when a family member, a father or mother, died. The interviewer never mentioned death and did not even hint at it. The question that initiated this virtually unanimous response was, "Tell me what happened when your spouse's communication led you to a deeper feeling of emotional intimacy?" The couples understood that "communication" meant more than just "speaking." The question was open-ended and not suggestive. These couples often took time to think about their responses to other questions, but when it came to this question there was no hesitation and an immediate answer about the death of a family member was provided. The one couple who did not mention the death of a family member, also thought about "death" as they instantly replied that they did not yet have any death in the family. What caused them to think of this response? Did they anticipate that such an experience would rouse their emotional intimacy?

It is interesting and striking to discover that being supported during a time of crisis is as important to adults as it is to children. Perhaps it speaks of a universal human need, awakened and stirred during these critical times.

The "big bang" impact on their emotional intimacy was not the death of a family member itself, but rather the spouse's support or lack thereof during the crisis. When the husband lost a parent he assessed the wife's support of him during that time. A favorable assessment led to tremendous growth of emotional intimacy. These couples reported that they had never felt closer to each other than when being supported by a spouse in a time of death. This closeness was not just felt by the supported spouse, but also by the supportive spouse. When a spouse lost a family member and did not feel supported by his or her spouse emotional intimacy disintegrated enormously. Support or lack thereof during a time of crisis truly had an enormous or "big bank" impact on emotional intimacy, either stimulating it, or destroying it.

Exactly as the child asks the question of the caregiver whether he or she is available and attending to the child during a crisis, danger or threat, so a spouse asks the same question. If the answer is affirmative, emotional intimacy is raised dramatically. Profound and meaningful attachment and bonding takes place. If the answer to that question is negative, emotional intimacy is trodden under foot, and attachment and bonding are shattered. The person in need of support then often withdraws. If the answer to that question is tentative and hesitant, "maybe sometimes and sometimes not" one would feel empty, uncertain and frustrated. The child and the spouse would try harder to turn tentative answers into affirmative answers and irregular affirmative answers, "sometimes", into reliable affirmative answers, "regularly", by making an effort to be more attached and bonded so that when the next crisis comes they would be closer together and then the answer would be more favorable.

Experiencing death in the family may be mentioned because of its enormous effect on emotional intimacy, but our responses during any kind of crisis effects emotional intimacy perhaps just the same, but with less result. Less significant effects on emotional intimacy are just less perceptible than the major effects, but they nonetheless accumulate. Whenever people experience a crisis, any crisis, they evaluate the response of others close to them. That measurement causes emotional intimacy between them to grow or to shrink. The brain uses a very complex "calculation model" to determine to what extent emotional intimacy should grow or shrink. The severity of the crisis determines the significance given to the response. A small crisis' response is valued less than a major crisis, for example, a death. Hence, response to a death experience has a massive effect on emotional intimacy, whereas a response to having "a bad day at work" has a smaller effect. The closeness or intimacy of the relationship also regulates the calculation.

The closer a person is to you the more that person's response to your crisis influences the emotional intimacy between you. If some unimportant random person does not support you during a crisis it does not have a major impact on the emotional intimacy between you two; the reason is that you were not expecting support anyway. The lack of support from people close to you, however, would cause you to doubt whether they were really close to you after all, and if they were really close to you, do they deserve to be? The attachment would be no longer certain and secure. Emotional intimacy would have been negatively affected. Of course the same is true on the positive side if support during a crisis was forthcoming.

The surefire way to improve emotional intimacy between you and your spouse is to be supportive during a time of crisis. Your support during a time of major crisis will increase your emotional intimacy in a major way, but supporting your spouse during a great number of little crises, indeed, even a "bad day" experience, adds up to bolster and sustain emotional intimacy between you.

Responses during a crisis, and this applies to any crisis including a perceived crisis, influences emotional intimacy much more than attempts to stimulate emotional intimacy when there is no crisis. Men need to feel that their spouses have taken "their side", and they do not want "advice." They wish to be "cheered on." They wish to hear how well they have performed or are performing. Women wish to feel that they are understood, recognized and appreciated. They do not wish to be told what to do, and they do not wish their spouses to do something on their behalf, for example, grieving and coping emotionally, if that was possible; this could not be done and it would not work. Women wish to know that you are identifying with their hurt, indeed, that you are "hurting with them", that is "sharing" their hurt. A great way to build up emotional intimacy is "to seek out" crises and regard them as opportunities to enhance emotional intimacy between you by being especially supportive during crises. Blaming and remarks, for example, "I told you so" reduce emotional intimacy, whereas support improves it.

Emotional intimacy can grow from almost nothing to remarkable closeness in one vast experience of feeling supported during a time of major crisis. Many couples got married after experiencing a major crisis together, even though they did not even know each other prior to that crisis. This happens all the time.

Emotional intimacy, however, can also disappear in one impressive and enormous moment if no support is provided or experienced, or if the support was less than expected. How many couples have you heard of breaking up right after a major crisis because one of them did not provide the needed and wanted support? In fact, this happens typically even before the crisis is over, often accompanied by a great deal of drama with a melodramatic and unashamed announcement that it is over. A measurement of emotional intimacy can be made by asking yourself how well and how often do you support your spouse during crises, regardless of the magnitude or severity of the crisis. It is easy to recognize a major crisis and to provide major support during that crisis. Indeed, that will have a major positive effect on emotional intimacy between the two of you. A huge price will be paid, however, if little crises are ignored and the spouse is not supported, as this inattention and negligence would have a major negative accumulative effect on emotional intimacy. A great deal of emotional intimacy could be gained by becoming a "detective" seeking for opportunities to provide support regardless of how insignificant and small those opportunities might be. *A major key to emotional intimacy is support during a crisis; a minor key is the consistency thereof.*

Now it is not suggested that you kill your mother-in-law in order to create a crisis wherein you can support your spouse and thereby gain emotional intimacy. Just be on the lookout for when your spouse is experiencing a crisis, any crisis or any magnitude. Offer support and be there for your spouse during these times.

Joe and Mary, have been married for seventeen years. Both rated their marriage favorably. Joe described the words "emotional intimacy" as the ability to share all his thoughts and feelings with Mary. Mary defined emotional intimacy as being "best friends" and sharing everything with Joe. Joe did not experience a great deal of emotional intimacy in the home where he grew up. He attempted to increase his emotional intimacy with Mary by way of touch, "slowing down" and focusing on her, having "date nights", and sending her love notes. She communicated feelings of emotional closeness with him by sending text messages during the day to ascertain how he is doing, and by spending time in the evening with him, talking. Both of them thought that these were good ways of building up emotional intimacy. Most people also think so. These ways of stimulating emotional intimacy only provide little "sparks" or stimuli, and they are certainly not "big bang" ways of providing rapid growth in emotional intimacy. She was asked to look back on their entire marriage and to describe the time when she felt most disconnected from Joe. Perhaps it would have been when he would have been too busy to slow down and focus on her, or maybe that they would have had no date night for some time and that no notes would have been sent. What would she select as the time when she felt most severely disconnected from Joe? What led to her feeling of disconnectedness during that time?

Her face had a somber expression as she stated that she felt mostly disconnected from Joe just after her mother had passed away. It was a difficult time in his career with a great number of events going on. He was physically away and deployed overseas at the time, leaving her feeling that he was not there for her, or supporting her. Obviously, it seemed as if he did not have a choice in the matter. It was rather interesting that her disconnectedness did not result from the lack of date nights or notes or anything else, but because of the lack of feeling supported during a time of crisis. In Mary and Joe's case the "big bang" or major effect on their emotional intimacy was negative. It resulted in feelings of disconnectedness. Joe spoke up and mentioned that Mary was there for him, and did it "very well", when his father passed away years before the time. Both of them reported that at the time of the death of Joe's father was a period that brought them closer together in a major way.

Experiencing death is a major crisis, hence, the spike or precipice in emotional intimacy during such times. Other crises can also create huge swings in emotional intimacy. Remember that the severity of the crisis determines the amount of swing, while the support of a spouse or lack thereof determines the direction of the swing, positively or negatively, in emotional intimacy.

Dan and Anne, were engaged. Both were living in California at the time. A great opportunity opened up for Dan to work on the East Coast. He resigned from his job and terminated all his contracts. His move to the East Coast went well. During the next few months they worked out the details of their long-distance relationship. Dan, however, became unhappy on the East Coast and things did not seem to go well. Before long he could not take it there anymore and decided to quit his job and move back to Anne and California; but there was a problem. He was moving back to nothing else but Anne. He had no job and had terminated all his California contracts. Furthermore, he had no home and they were on the verge of getting married. How was he going to support a family? What was he going to do and where was he going to find a new job? He experienced a crisis.

In response to Dan's crisis Anne flew to the East Coast just to hop right into his car for the long drive back to California with him. They talked all the way. She was there for him during his crisis. He felt supported and did not face his crisis alone; she encouraged him. She pointed out how talented he was and that he would soon find a job. Now, some twenty years later, Dan was asked about a time in their relationship when he felt the closest to Anne. Both of them rated their marriage and the closeness between them very favorably. They described themselves as best friends. Both of them have had and continue to have wonderful careers. Their children are flourishing. They were a happy family. Dan had many events on his mind, covering twenty years of marriage, to choose from to select a time or event when he felt the closest to Anne. Instantly, seemingly without even thinking to weigh up all the wonderful times they have shared, Dan picked this story of Anne supporting him during his crisis as the time when he felt the closest to her. This experience even topped the experiences of the birth of their children in his estimation of its impact on their emotional intimacy. She did not spend a lot of money on Dan. She did not "do" anything "great" for Dan. She was simply there for him during his crisis. Yet, that simple action propelled their emotional intimacy into orbit.

Yes, the "big bang" or immense influence on emotional intimacy is support, or lack thereof, during any time of major crises. Support during minor crises also provides more "bang for the buck" or inspiration for growth in emotional intimacy than any other means. A crisis may be a challenging time in life, but it is also a great opportunity to increase emotional intimacy. The worse the crisis the greater is the opportunity to foster emotional intimacy. Some may be tempted to think that they don't have to do anything but sit and wait for a crisis to appear before springing into action to stimulate emotional intimacy. That is not the case as the best result comes from consistent and regular support. Inconsistent support does not stimulate a healthy and Secure Attachment style, but causes preoccupation with attachment that is less healthy for the relationship. The best guidance regarding the generation of emotional intimacy is to seek out all crises, vast or small, to be consistently there for your spouse. If you pay extra attention when it is a major crisis it would yield even more profound rewards.

For support to be most beneficial, to increase emotional intimacy, one has to remember that the concept "support" means different things to the different genders. Women feel more supported when someone listens to them, shares their pain and helps them to feel understood. They wish to share their crisis experience. Attaining solutions or attempting to resolve things for women is not equated with "feeling supported." For men the word "support" means to be encouraged, reassured, and to be "cheered on." They wish to be on top when they come out on the other side of the crisis. Men do not regard feeling their pain and sharing their experiences as being supportive. Support and building up of a husband as a person are most advantageous for him. Supporting his decisions is highly valued when you agree, and it may be wise to not say anything if you disagree, unless being silent would have negative consequences. Men need to know that you are on "their side", fighting this crisis along with them.

For a magnificent or "surefire" spark there is no "bigger bang" or immense inspiration than consistent support in a time of crisis. It would be unwise and even "foolish" to let those opportunities go by without supporting your spouse. Should you wish to ignite a "surefire spark" or a warm glow in your emotional intimacy, just provide support to your spouse in a crisis, and make it known that you are there for him or her, supporting your spouse, and that you would always be there for him or her in future.

⚓ CHAPTER FOUR ⚓

EMPATHY: MISFIRE OR SUREFIRE?

To support a partner during a crisis is the huge or "big bang" influence on emotional intimacy. A crisis forces us to sacrifice issues that distract from the relationship, and to focus intensely on the needs of the spouse going through the crisis. During a crisis we seem more authentic and genuine. We are in harmony with each other's feelings; we spend more time talking about these feelings and we open up to each other. There seems to be an authenticity in the air, a type of unconditional and unqualified atmosphere during a crisis. Then we are inclined to be willing to contribute, to support and to love without expecting anything in return. This is love in its purest form and it is very attractive. A crisis by its very nature often requires unconditional compassion and empathy. Empathy is different than sympathy and more resilient than sympathy, and it is also more powerful in bringing about emotional intimacy. When couples support each other in crises they are experiencing empathy to some extent. Experiencing empathy can be used to measure the level of emotional support between people, especially in the case of women.

As in the case of emotional intimacy, men express and show empathy in a specific way; the male "empathy language", while women articulate it in their particular way; the female "empathy language." Women are partly "bilingual" as they are able to also understand the male empathy language. Men are not able to understand the female empathy language. Very young children can understand what we say even though they cannot speak yet. Similarly, women understand what men express without being able to articulate empathy in the male empathy language themselves.

Men can articulate their way of expressing empathy, but they are totally oblivious of, and clueless regarding women's way of expressing empathy and their empathy "language." These two ways of articulating empathy are like two different "languages" for men, as they are not even related to one another, but totally foreign.

When a woman receives empathy from a man she entertains it in his way or "language", because he provides empathy; and he can only articulate it in his one way or one "language"; a man's style or kind of empathy! Since she is "semi-bilingual" or partly experiences more than one way of appreciating empathy, she is able to comprehend and understand it, though she cannot express or "speak" it. The conclusion is that women appreciate men's empathy due to their ability to understand the males' way of articulating empathy or their way of "speaking empathy language."

The research confirmed that women had experienced empathy from their husbands. The women felt comforted and experienced a deeper level of solidarity and camaraderie between them and their husbands; they felt that their spouses experienced their pain together with them. Husbands and wives identified with each other and felt closer to each other as a result. It should be noted here that the empathy experienced by women from men is not as effective as the empathy experienced by women *from women*, as they articulate empathy in the same way or "speak" the same "empathy language." The male's way of conveying empathy or his empathy "language" is not understood by women as well as they comprehend their own way or follow their own "language"; nevertheless, when men empathize with women it is recognized, comprehended and appreciated.

Men, on the other hand, are not able to comprehend different languages of empathy, or to follow cross-gendered ways of articulating empathy, or understand the female empathy "language." Men have no idea what women express or "say" when women attempt to empathize with them. To make matters worse, the words and concepts used by women to empathize with men, using female "empathy language", sound like "curse" words according to male empathy "language." So, instead of experiencing empathy, men actually feel "cursed", or that bad "language" has been used against them, and they have been rejected. The women do not actually "curse" them, they simply attempt to display empathy, but the men do not understand their approach and "words", and they understand and "hear" expressions, sounding like "curse words', according to their own empathy "language." A disastrous result is that men, more often than not, do not experience empathy when their wives articulate it. They feel as if their spouses treat them humiliatingly.

Years ago my wife and I were looking to buy a house. We had more taste than money, because the houses in our price range were far below our taste range. One realtor attempted her very best to make cheaper homes appeal to us, but I heard something different from what she conveyed. She said the house was "pleasant and cozy"; I heard that the house was "real tiny." She said that a specific house "needed some love"; I heard that this house was "dilapidated." She said that yet another house's color scheme felt more "restful and calm"; I heard that the house was too "dark." She said that a different house's color scheme was "lively and vibrant"; I could almost hear myself ask, "Where are my sunglasses?" She said that another house was in an "established neighborhood"; I heard that the house was in an "ancient neighbor-hood." At long last we could not match our taste with our money and did not buy a home at that time. It all turned out providential in the end as the housing crisis struck a few years later and home prices plummeted, and consequently, we bought a house we really loved.

Empathy flowing from a woman to a man sounds pretty much like the conversation between the realtor and I. She was trying her best to be agreeable and to empathize with my disappointment. She saw things in a positive light, but I heard a different story. I heard that my taste was wrong, that I needed to change my expectations, that the problem was not significant and that all I had to do was to "deal with reality."

Like the very first realtor, women are inclined to communicate empathy by letting their husbands know that everything will work out just fine in the end by saying things like, "If you painted the house a different color it would really be a nice house." Women attempt to communicate to men that they are with them in the crisis by mentioning, for example, "Our first house was also a pleasant little starter home."

Words like "we are in the same boat" are used, for example. When they utter these words, women attempt to bond with their husbands. Women share a similar experience in an attempt to make a connection between him and her, just like the first realtor wanted to create a connection between us by sharing with us that her first house was also small. Shared experiences, however, are more valuable to women than men. Male empathy "language" and ways of expressing it does not follow this method or use these kinds of words in these situations. Rather, males' ways of expressing empathy and these types of words in these situations, requiring empathy, sound very similar to "negative" concepts.

Consequently, it is not surprising that men do not hear the same constructive and positive messages as women intended to communicate. Men are inclined to "hear" negative and destructive messages. Remember that the concept "support" means different things to the two genders. It is as if they are spoken in totally different empathy "languages." The researcher asked women what they had said to demonstrate empathy. Later, men were asked how these messages made an impact on them. The purpose of the research was to determine whether the women's intent of empathy was successful regarding their husbands.

Regardless of what the women actually said, the men stated that they were of the opinion that the wives were not focused on the problem. Men are solution-oriented and they want issues to be resolved. Women are relationally oriented and want to set up networks between people to connect with them. The wives are focused on relationships, attachments and togetherness, while men are focused on the problem at hand. Attachments and togetherness for men are not going to solve the issue. The men reported hearing negative messages, for example, "Just suck it up", and "Just get over it." Men interpret their wives' consolation, for example, "I have had that happen to me before" as saying, "I have dealt with it before, why can't you deal with it now?" The study disclosed that it was typical that men found it difficult to enjoy empathy from their wives, and as a result do not often experience empathy. When a man is encouraged and "cheered on" when facing a crisis requiring empathy, he feels more suitable to take on the problem. He then feels as if she wishes him to win and that she believes that he can succeed. Now, that makes foolproof or "surefire" sense in male empathy utterances or "language."

A great deal of male communication involves the topic of "rivalry" and "competition" in one form or another. When men stand around telling their stories they are "competing" to see who has the best story. At work men are often trying to surpass or exceed others. Yes, they laugh and enjoy stories, but while the laugher is going on their minds work overtime to come up with something better to say. If they do not succeed in this, their next story, joke or anecdote may well be at the expense of someone else in the group. The thinking behind this phenomenon may often well be, "If I cannot be better, I must let him be worse."

So when a man is going through a crisis and a woman tells her story of her crisis to bond with him and to share the experience, the man regards her story as "competing" with his story. Her empathy "language" regards her expressions as bonding two lives. According to his empathy "language" she just attempts to surpass him. He typically feels that the purpose of her story is to indicate that his crisis is not such a big problem. He cannot understand why she, who is supposed to be on his side, to support him, would try either to one-up him, or to show that his crisis is not as bad as what she has experienced. This is exactly the opposite for a man who wished to be supported. She, on the other hand, thinks that her "language" of empathy is going to be a major or "surefire" success in causing him to feel her empathy. After all, that is what she would have wished to hear if she was in such a crisis. Instead, it turns out to be a failure or a "misfire" because their empathy "languages" differ completely.

Women empathize with their spouses with what would be a certain or "surefire" way of empathizing with other ladies. Men experience this type of attempt as blame, a statement of not being worthy or good enough. Instead of failing or "misfiring" with what women think would be a convincing or "surefire" success, women would be better off by focusing on assisting them to find solutions. This, however, does not come naturally to women when they deal with relational issues. They may need some practice to start thinking this way.

Men generally observe the problem rather than the relationship. Men have reported that they would find it more helpful if women were to discuss various options to resolve issues rather than attempting to "sugarcoat" issues or make the concerns seem less unpleasant. Whether or not these suggested options regarding empathy are viable solutions are irrelevant. It is more important for men to see that women are on their side. The concept "on his side" in the male empathy understanding or "language" means that "they", he and his wife, are fighting the crisis together, or at least he is being supported in the fight, rather than that their past shared experiences join them together on the "same side," or that they are on the same side by virtue of shared experiences.

Men experience emotional intimacy better if they feel genuine empathy from their wives, according to their understanding. This task would be better achieved by not even mentioning any crises of your own as a woman when attempting to convey empathy. Admiration of his "courage and strength" to face the issue is more important as a part of the male empathy "vocabulary" than anecdotes. A man wishes to hear his wife voice her support of how he has dealt with the situation so far if possible, and how he managed in the past, if not possible to say of the current event. What enhances a man's satisfaction, empathizing with him, is her focus on the issue that he faces and her focus on him as a person. She can assist him and he will interpret it as empathy if she assists him "to clarify the issues."

When empathy is required due to some problems, men love a "brain-storming" partner, or to consider with him all possibilities in a creative way. Men love to be "cheered on." A man needs to feel that his spouse backs him up, supports, and endorses him. He needs to feel that his spouse supports what he is planning and intending to do, if possible. If she does not support what he is planning to do or criticizes his plan, it will drain all empathy and emotional intimacy as he will feel criticized as a person rather than that she only criticized his plan of action.

When men sense any form of criticism, most of them have a hard time to distinguish whether such criticism is targeting him as a person or his action plans. Men almost always take criticism personally: Remember the "competition outlook" of men. Criticism in male "language" or in a man's approach means that the criticizer, expressing disapproval or dissatisfaction, is opposing him, is against him, and is, therefore, a competitor or an enemy. Men have a hard time equating such an interpretation with empathy. This misunderstanding, however, is not the women's fault, or responsibility. No one is to be blamed. Men and women just have two different languages of expressing empathy: One for men and one for women. This is just the way it is. Men will be better off not to regard their wives as their enemies or opposition parties. Most women really care and are indeed very empathetic. The "language" barrier simply prevents men from seeing it. A man appreciates his spouse assisting him to find a solution, and he values a complimenting partner to tackle the issue together with him to come up with more options. When he realizes that she is on his side, working with him to solve the problem, he experiences empathy. Minimizing the problem, however, minimizes his perception of empathy. If the issue is not fixable or solutions are impossible (such as in the case of a death) men just want to hear how well they are doing and how their wives admire them.

Men would be better off if they realize that their wives do not mean to put them down. They just happen to value togetherness more than being solution-oriented. They try to tell men that they are not alone and that they are actually experience their agony with them. It may not solve the problem, but remember, feeling alone and isolated is "torture" to a woman; wives don't want their spouses to feel "tortured." Men and women just "speak" different empathy" languages", or have different ways of conveying empathy, which is not always understood as empathy by the other gender. Even though her empathy "language" sounds like "curse words" in the man's empathy "language" or communication it does not mean that they are intended as "curse words"; they are really intended to create bonding, togetherness, and solidarity.

Women would feel even more empathy from their men if they knew that "presenting solutions" is a male way of conveying empathy or his empathy "language." Men reason that the best way "to stop the suffering" is "to solve the problem." When men attempt to solve a problem or to provide a solution their purpose is to discontinue the hurt because they don't want their spouses to hurt. Empathy only fails or "misfires" as long as we do not learn each other's way of conveying empathy or "empathy language." Empathy can inspire us every time if we understand and comprehend each other's thinking and action with regard to empathy. Experiencing empathy is an important way of feeling supported during crises. Learning to convey each other's way of empathy or to "speak" each other's empathy "languages" will go a long way to assist us to feel more supported, and thereby, to enhance emotional intimacy.

Another certain or "surefire" way to assist a spouse to feel empathy is by using "body language" and facial expressions. All the interviewed couples of both genders indicated that facial expressions communicated empathy effectively. To comprehend and understand how the different genders think about empathy will at least teach us a few ways to convey empathy to the other gender or to understand "words" of the other gender's strange empathy "language." If the opposite gender's way of empathy or empathy "language" is grasped we would be able to recognize their attempts to empathize with us. Moreover, if we can learn not only to understand the other gender's way of empathy or "language", but actually learn to convey or "speak" it, and also learn to act accordingly, we would cause emotional intimacy to grow by using this wonderful tool, called empathy, more efficiently. Whether empathy "misfires", or whether it succeeds or "surefires", depends on our ability to "compel" or "constrain" ourselves to think the same as the opposite gender using their mindset and their empathy language rather than our own. Our ability to experience empathy depends on our ability to enhance, improve and develop ourselves to recognize their attempts to empathize with us.

✄ CHAPTER FIVE ✄

TRUTH AND TRUST

Women might have a more difficult task to communicate empathy effectively than do men. Men, however, might have a more difficult task to deal with truth more than do women. The specific aim of the previous chapter is to assist women to understand men (in terms of empathy), whereas this chapter is especially aimed at aiding men to understand and work with women.

Emotional intimacy for women has to do with opening up and showing their emotions and sentiments reserved for people with whom they are emotionally intimate and with whom they share their secrets. Women feel "punished", lonely and isolated when they are not allowed into the privacy of intimate feelings and sentiments. Almost nothing can be worse for women than exclusion from another's heart. Being lied to, for women, however, is worse than exclusion; it is exclusion combined with deception.

For the past twelve years I observed boys and girls playing at school on a weekly basis; I served as a chaplain for an elementary school and I now volunteer teach for a high school. Boys and girls play completely differently. Boys always seem to be involved in some kind of competition. Instead of competing, girls tend to collaborate.

Girls are often found on the playground, whispering into each other's ears, and showing possessions to each other. Friendships among girls are fostered and measured by the depth and frequency of sharing secrets. When they share their secrets it is an invitation to friendship and trust. The more secretive and private the secrets are that is being shared the deeper and more intimate the friendship became.

When boys get mad at each other they attempt to win the "competition"; fighting is also a form of competition. When girls get mad at each other they "exclude" each other. Playground-chatter among girls, reflecting discord, might be identified by phrases such as, "I would not tell you my secrets", "you cannot come to my party", or "we would not play with you." Sharing secrets among girls measures the closeness of friendships. Girls interpreted exclusion as punishment.

These observations, however, are not new. Many scholars have written at length about the topic. Please consult the following publication for more information on these remarks: Tannen, Deborah, He said, she said: Exploring the different ways men and women communicate. Barnes & Noble. Audio. 2004.

When boys play, it soon turns out to be a game with winners and losers. When they play as a team, they are very protective of those on their team. Boys shield those who were battling on their side. To battle together against a common "enemy" develops friendships among boys. It is also not uncommon for boys, who are on the same team battling together a short while ago, to be skirmishing against each other later on. When an opposing player points a finger at a boy on the other team his fellow team members get involved very quickly, almost always to defend and to protect the accused boy. When boys grow up they still believe that it is their duty to protect those on "their team."

In marriage women view the sharing of secrets as a relationship-building tool, resulting in great emotional intimacy. In marriage a man regards the protection of his wife and family as one of his core duties and obligations. Most men would sacrifice their own lives to protect their wives and families. Women often think of this protective mindset of men in terms of physical protection. What they are not aware of is that men also do their very best to protect their women and families from other burdens, such as worries. When things go wrong for a man, the "male mindset" wishes to protect his wife and family from worrying. Men wish to protect their wives from carrying the burdens they have to carry. This protective mindset is equally strong with regard to both physical and emotional protection. Men think that they are doing their wives a tremendous service by not sharing things that may cause them to carry emotional burdens.

So Mr. Right, not referring to a real person, ascertains that there would be another round of layoffs at work. Rumor has it that he might be on the list from which one third would be selected for dismissal. The final decision would be made known in three months' time. Mr. Right is worried, but his need to protect his wife from worrying, a kind of "pain", prevents him from telling her. After all, only one third of the people on the list would lose their jobs. Perhaps he would not be one of those; he aims "to win this competition" for his job and then he would tell his wife, or else he would cause her a great deal of unnecessary concern. He wishes to do anything possible to protect her from emotional pain, for example, worry. He regards it as his problem and he should fix it. He thinks that he needs to do anything possible to protect his wife from experiencing all the negative feelings that he is required to deal with. He regards this as the proper thing to do as it is a man's task "to protect" his wife.

For the last two months Mrs. Right has suspected that something was wrong. Mr. Right appeared more quiet than usual. It has been as if he was distracted. It appeared as though he was "not there" even though he was physically present. She has been prying and nagging him to find out what was wrong. Not that she was nosy, but he had a secret and she regarded the sharing of a secret as an opportunity for enhancing emotional intimacy. Secrets are supposed to be shared by intimate friends (according to women). Since he does not share what bothers him she now feels left out and "punished" by exclusion. She experiences heartache in the relationship. She interprets the situation as women would normally construe it; she now regards him not to be so close to her as she would have hoped for, or perhaps she regards him as not trusting her with his secret.

Finally, the news is somehow broken; he might lose his job. He feels bad that she is now concerned and worried as he regards this as his failure to protect her. He sees the anguish on her face and blames himself for it. On the other hand, she cannot understand what she has done wrong to deserve this "punishment" (exclusion) from him, as it was he that excluded her from such an important issue and secret. Why did he not share his secret with her? Unwillingness to share secrets is regarded by her as evidence that they do not have a special relationship; if he were close to her he would have shared the secret: In fact, that is what close friends do, according to her. Mr. Right thought, on the other hand, that he protected her from bearing the burden. Mrs. Right, however, feels excluded and "punished." Both of them are now confused. He cannot understand why she is upset as he protected her from being upset during the last two months. She cannot understand why he would not share his secrets with her. Why would a husband exclude his wife "for no reason at all"?

His need to protect her seems to be in conflict with her need to be included and to be trusted with his secret. He thinks mistakenly that her concern would "kill the fire" of the relationship. She thinks erroneously that lack of sharing his secret means that the "fire" of the relationship is already dampened, or else he would have shared his secret. The reality, however, is that he has been attempting to protect her, on the one hand, and that on the other hand, she has a need to be included in his secret, especially about something so important.

Men feel the need to protect their wives, as that is what men are supposed to do. Whether women like it or not that protection includes protection from emotional "hurt" according to men. When a woman asks a question and the answer may "hurt" her, according to the man, he finds himself in an awkward position. Does he tell his wife the truth, but hurt her? Or does he evade the true story and protect her from "hurt"?

When a woman tries on a new dress, for example, and asks her husband how she looks in an expecting and excited tone of voice, he finds himself in just such an awkward position. He can see how excited she looks; her eyes look so happy and she is expecting a positive reply. It is rather obvious that she likes the dress. Indeed, if he finds the new dress attractive he is off the hook; but the beads of sweat begin to roll if he dislikes the dress. He faces a choice: Honesty would mean "hurt" to her, and dishonesty would not mean "damage" to her. The more he loves her, the stronger his need to protect her from "pain." The "default", automatic inclination for most men would be to choose protection; "distorting the facts" or even "lying" is the price they have to pay to purchase the protection from hurt. Men discern this as a necessary evil, the cost for true love. I am not defending this behavior, rather just explaining its basis.

Besides being wrong, there is another extensive problem with men "lying", as they are typically not that good at it. Somehow, women sense when men lie, they see right through it, especially when it has to do with intimacy. When this happens she feels deceived and betrayed. She experiences that he has violated her trust and that their emotional intimacy has been shattered. He thinks that he has been protecting her from "hurt", but this very act of protection has caused pain, severe pain, the kind of anguish that takes a long time to heal. This pain exceeds by far the pain she would have felt if he just told the truth in the first place. Women desire that men would learn that the choice of protection from emotional pain is not between pain on the one hand and no pain on the other. They see it rather as a choice of pain with the truth, and worse pain with a lie. Given these two options, the better choice for men would be to choose the option with the least amount of pain; the truth, that is true protection.

David and Amy had been married for over twenty years when we talked about the following incident. One afternoon some friends from work invited David to travel with them to a neighboring town. No one could remember why the "boys" went that day to the neighboring town. Even worse, none could remember exactly to which neighboring town they travelled. As David told Amy that he was going with the "boys" he mentioned that he would come back home at approximately 6:30 p.m. When it was 6:30 p.m. Amy had dinner ready. She always had dinner ready at approximately that time. For many years they had eaten together as a family. That day David was late. At seven o'clock there was still no sign of him. At seven thirty Amy started becoming upset. Perhaps you would say, "Yes, I know, I would also have been upset a lot earlier." Recounting the experience, Amy said, "Come on, there was a phone; you could have called if you were going to be late." That call, however, came hours later. By this time Amy was furious. She asked him at what time he would be home, and his answer was, "Well, I don't know." This reply was just not good enough for Amy. As she tried to obtain more information the phone simply went dead. Perhaps his cell phone lost its signal – who could tell? She waited about five minutes in the hope that he would regain a cell phone signal, and when he did not call her back, she called him again. David, however, did not answer her call. Amy called David's cell phone every five minutes, but his cell phone simply went straight into voice mail.

By this time, Amy knew to which town David went; it was a fairly large town with good cell phone reception. Consequently, she knew that it would not take long to regain cell phone reception. Her anger turned into worry. Was something wrong? Was David okay? A couple of hours passed; her worry turned back into anger. She thought that he had simply turned off his cell phone because he did not wish to talk to her; this could be "punishment" by "exclusion." She thought that he did not wish to explain himself to her. She was certain that he did not wish to face her wrath. She was convinced that he was having a good time with the "boys", that he simply did not wish to speak to her, and that he was "excluding" her. The more she thought about him, enjoying himself, the angrier she became. It was as if her anger was proportionate to her estimation of his enjoyment, although she had no basis to make such a guesstimate. Why did David not answer her questions when he phoned the first time? Why did he not know what time he would be home? She concluded that David was hiding something from her. What if David went to a place she disapproved of? By this time she was certain that David was lying to her. She ended her story by recounting that this event "was just devastating" to her. Her emotional intimacy was worn out.

David did not get home until midnight or one o'clock; neither of them could remember the exact time. We do not have to guess what the topic of discussion has been the next day. Among other things, David was accused of lying. Up to this point Amy was telling the story. Now David began telling his side of the story of what happened. He began by denying all her accusations. He acknowledged that he came home a great deal later than anticipated. He was out with the "boys" and having a good time. He did not remember that he had to call Amy about coming home late until it was way too late. David did not realize that to women, and consequently, to Amy the fact that she was not remembered and that he was not concerned to think of her was already a negative force draining her emotional intimacy. In any case, he called her when he remembered to do so. He had nothing to hide. They were not in some "forbidden" place. They were not doing anything wrong or questionable. He could not answer her questions because they did not plan to go out that evening. They simply decided on the spur of the moment what to do and where to go. As David and Amy were speaking during that first phone call, David's cell phone battery went flat and his phone turned off. He was the only one in the group with a cell phone. It was not true that he did not wish to take her phone calls. It was not true that he turned off his cell phone deliberately. No matter what David said, he was not successful in persuading her of his "innocence." As far as Amy was concerned David "lied"; David strongly contested this accusation as he was being truthful. At present, a few years later, she still believes that David has "lied" that night, and David still insists that he has been telling the truth.

So, why did Amy not believe David? David was not in the habit of going out with the "boys"; this was a very rare event. He has never been unfaithful. He has never been in questionable places. He does not use any alcohol. He is not known for being late. Many couples find themselves in the same situation. The husband would be willing to undertake a polygraph or a lie detector test, but the wife would still not believe him. Many men could be ready to testify on David's behalf, but she would still not believe him. The reason is very simple; David was caught lying to her before. Her trust was violated. Being lied to by someone with whom a woman shares emotional intimacy is a painful and a rarely forgotten event. This anguish runs deep. To protect her from more pain she has to push him away to some extent. The closer people are to each other the higher the potential reward of love and bonding; but the reverse is equally true. The closer people are to each other the more severe the pain when there is relational anguish. Relationships are all about "rewards" (love) and "risks" (pain). When she pushes him away to protect herself from the pain and to punish him by exclusion for what he did or did not do, emotional intimacy suffers the loss. People can protect themselves very effectively against relational pain, but at the cost of sacrificing the reward of love. It is not possible to have it both ways.

Both the husband and wife now have a problem. She is anguished because of his "lie" and consequently, she would not believe him again. He has a problem because there is nothing he can do to convince her otherwise. The only thing that he can do is to be truthful every time about everything; over a long, long time he can regain her trust. In the meantime she would not believe him, no matter what. As untruthfulness ruins a woman's trust and drains her emotional intimacy, "not being able to fix things" drives men "crazy." Men are all about finding solutions and fixing things. Now he faces a situation where he is not trusted to tell the truth, which he cannot do anything about. When a man comes to the realization that there is absolutely nothing he can do that will make a difference, he will give up. When he gives up he also shuts down his emotional intimacy. He might not say anything, but the relationship would be disintegrating and "dying." He would live with his wife and he might even be pleasant to her, but there would be hardly any emotional intimacy left. Would both husband and wife not have been better off without that first "lie"? I could almost hear this agreement from the lady readers, but it is not that simple for men. For them to agree they have to deny their role as protectors.

There is a better option, however; when we learn that this kind of protection causes her more severe pain than what it is supposed to prevent, it makes men rethink the situation, doesn't it? The imposition of more pain equals a greater failure of protection than the lesser pain that the truth presents. The pain with the truth is only the pain of the relevant situation, which he faces. The pain with the lie is the combined pain of both the situation plus the damaged relationship, caused by the "lie." In most cases men would not be able to protect their wives from finding out what bothers them in the first place. It would tend to be only a matter of time anyway before she would find out. I do not know about your mother, but my mother just knew when I was up to something. If mothers simply know when their children would be facing an issue, then what makes men think that their wives do not notice the same thing when they suffer something? Do not ask me how, but women just know, period!

The problem of wives not believing men because of a previous "lie" is very common among couples.

Let's move on to another story; he was trying to communicate emotional intimacy to smooth over an argument. She suspected that he was paying too much attention to someone else. It was no more than a suspicion. Now, a few years later she confirmed that she was wrong about that fight; he had never paid too much attention to any other lady and she had been his only love.

Please listen how Christopher voiced his frustration when he was not believed to be telling the truth; "it was frustrating, no matter what I said or did, nothing helped; she had a block and would not even listen to me." Christopher was convinced that she was not even giving him a chance. It was as if she had already "made up her mind" about his guilt before he spoke. That incident between them turned out badly, as he stopped the relationship for a week; this was just before they got married. Now, it would be easy for women simply to say that Christopher should not have told the first "lie", and then this problem would never have occurred. She would have believed him. This might very well be the case. This is the reason to plead to men to open up and to be honest and truthful with their wives at all times. At the same time, however, without diminishing what was just said, women also need to understand that these "lies" were never meant to be deceptive, neither were they always covering up something; they were intended to protect the wife from hurt and pain. Here I am not talking about a person blatantly attempting to hide misconduct. It is a "natural" male response to his need to protect her.

Women reading this section would probably be saying or thinking, "I do not need his protection", or "I can protect myself." That might also be true, but that is not how men usually think. Just as men can often not convince women that they are telling the truth, so women cannot convince men that they do not need to protect their women. Love and protection go hand in hand for men, the two concepts are inseparable; if you love, you will protect.

Christopher's wife said that she attempted to enhance emotional intimacy between them by nagging her husband "to get things out of him", "as he did not wish to talk about it." While she thought that she was increasing emotional intimacy he reported that she deflated his emotional intimacy, as "she would keep on asking; when I was not ready to reply, she would try to make me ready." While he thought that he was protecting her from hurt with the "lie" prior to this event, she felt depleted by his non-communication. Men might think that things they did exhausted their wives' emotional intimacy, but it is often what they did not do, or do not tell that saps their wives' emotional intimacy. This incident drained both of them.

Women require openness and honesty if their emotional intimacy is to be enhanced. Even the very hint of a lie from their husbands drains their emotional intimacy quickly and for a long time. Men, on the other hand, believe that they must protect their spouses from pain and "lying" might be necessary to do so. When they are caught out, however, men face a situation for which there is no short-term solution; even when telling the truth their wives would not believe them. If men would lie, how would their wives determine that they lied or told the truth? Therefore the safest route for them as women, to minimize hurt, is to take everything as a "lie" when the situation or body language warrants it. When women believe what men say and it turns out to be a lie the pain is worse than when an expected lie turns out to be a lie. Wives might even bring up a lie years after the fact. To men it seems as if there is no escape.

Husbands and wives continue to pay the price for a long time. He is not being believed even when telling the truth. She feels deceived and excluded, even betrayed. The research indicated that husbands felt that they were called hypocrites. Husbands voiced their frustration by saying that there was nothing they could do or say to convince their wives otherwise. Wives were frustrated because they did not know when to believe their husbands and when not to. Women do not wish to have serious relationships where they still need to ask the question of truthfulness.

Counterintuitive as it might feel, to not damage emotional intimacy men have to realize that "lying" is not only wrong, but a very ineffective way of protecting their wives' feelings. The benefit of not hurting a spouse is far outweighed by the damage and hurt caused when found out. A little hurt with honesty is much better than deep and long-term hurt with dishonesty.

Next to secrets shared honesty is what women use most to measure trust and the depth of emotional intimacy. Remember that women build up emotional intimacy by sharing secrets. Well, who is going to share secrets with someone who is not trustworthy? If women feel that they cannot share their secrets they have been robbed of one of the only ways they know of to enhance emotional intimacy. As a result emotional intimacy disintegrate and "dies." No matter what, the honest option is always going to cost less in the long run. The research indicated that wives required honesty and that lying has turned out for men to be a very frustrating and long-term problem to recover from. Women need to be included even if it hurts.

Please keep in mind that although crises hurt, they enhance emotional intimacy when they are accompanied by support. Similarly, truth binds a woman to a man even if that truth hurts. Of course there are exceptions; do not think that telling your wife about an affair is going to bind her to you; but also do not think that she will never find out.

When she finds out the pain will be worse than if she were told in the beginning. The pain will always be less when a story is told honestly than when it is found out later, after it was hidden. The reason is simple, women now need to deal not only with what happened, strike one, but also with the deception and lying, strike two, that went along with it; double strike equals double pain.

Men wish that women would know that their "lying" is often not to hide things, but to offer protection from hurt; not that that would make it right. When "lying" is used to hide things it is probably done because men believed that knowledge of what they were trying to hide would hurt her. When a man "lied" it might be good for both spouses to resolve the dishonesty issue and to put the issue to rest. Men long for women to stop clinging to the past. Men wish to move on. Now that is easy for a man to say. Women find it more difficult "to move on" for reasons we will not go into here. Disbelieving a husband in spite of evidence of his truthfulness will cause him to give up.

Husbands could be assisted effectively if wives learned not to ask them questions, which may have answers that the husbands might think could hurt their wives; for example, the eternal question:; "Do I look fat?" This could place a husband in an untenable position from which his mind could not find an escape. Many women might not understand a man's reasoning to regard "lying" as a means of protecting her from hurt. Let us ask the question, "Ladies, have other women ever told you that your clothing is 'ugly', or that a particular piece of clothing makes you look fat?" No, of course not. Why is it that women only receive positive remarks about their clothing from other women (negative remarks are couched positively)? The remarks would even be provided in such a way that the negative answer is perceived to be to the recipient's benefit. Negative remarks would only be given when women think it would bond and connect them to each other.; for example, a negative comment might save a women's face by telling her in private, before the others found out that a piece of clothing is unlatched. Negative remarks may positively convey that "I am looking out for your interests." Are all the compliments ladies receive from other ladies always true? Women complement each other as a means of connecting. Complements are cords provided from one woman to the next, enabling them to pull each other closer and consequently creating a bond. Just as women are over-enthusiastic to complement each other to be connected to one another, so men are overzealous to protect their wives. Whether it is twisting the truth or outright lying, it is often not maliciously intended.

Men, the research is clear; there is no other way, relationships with women demand truthfulness. Truthfulness protects them from worse pain. Openness, honesty, and sharing secrets will enhance their emotional intimacy towards you. They would readily volunteer to carry your burdens with you. To women that is a means of bonding. When there is an issue, whether it concerns them or not, if it bothers them, they wish to know about it. Regardless of intentions, the best policy is always honesty. A lot of heartache can be spared just by being truthful. Truth, honesty, and trust are central to emotional intimacy. Truth, honesty, and trust are foundational to surefire romantic relationships.

❧ CHAPTER SIX ❧

THE UNEXPECTED GIFT TO EMOTIONAL INTIMACY

Sometimes it is easier to understand something concrete and physical rather than to comprehend an abstract concept. Emotional intimacy is an abstract concept and as such it is more difficult to characterize, define, measure, and understand. It is one of those concepts that people know the meaning of, but when asked to describe and define it they have a difficult time to explain the meaning. To facilitate a better understanding of emotional intimacy it may be helpful in the first place, to look at a concrete and physical concept. Once that physical concept is understood a transition can be made to the abstract notion of emotional intimacy. Creating this "bridge" between the physical and the abstract may provide a different perspective that is easier to grasp. Let us consider "physical intimacy" to see what we can learn about "emotional intimacy" in the process.

A high percentage of the couples interviewed actually became confused between emotional intimacy and physical intimacy; so, there are definitely similarities between these two kinds of intimacies. As a result, we can ask, what is physical intimacy? How does the dynamics of physical intimacy between people work? People interact with each other on a daily basis; when are those interactions of an intimate nature? What is the difference between touching one another and intimate touch? Are there ways of being physically intimate without touching?

First, human interaction becomes intimate when it happens within each other's private space. No touch is then even necessary for interaction to be intimate; proximity by itself qualifies as intimacy. Physical intimacy occurs when people are allowed into each other's "personal space." When someone's face is right up to yours, even without touching, that is physical intimacy. When somebody shouts into another person's face, however, it is intruding the other person's private space, which indicates disregard for that person. Physical intimacy occurs in the personal space where other people in general are not allowed to be. More will be said later regarding personal space.

Second, the length of interaction between people can determine the level of physical intimacy. If someone holds on to another person's hand for longer than usual while shaking hands, it becomes intimate. Hence, a normal handshake is not considered intimate. Normal eye contact is not intimate when speaking, whilst holding eye contact longer than usual is a form of intimacy.

Third, the level of closeness granted can measure physical intimacy. Clothing hides intimate body parts. It is intimacy, however, if someone allows another person access to intimate parts, normally covered. Access can be allowed by touch or sight. The deepest level of physical intimacy is when nothing is held back and complete access is allowed.

Without the level of closeness required it is deemed inappropriate to enter another's private space, to touch physically for too long, and to gain access to parts where others are not allowed. A person is violated when an "unauthorized" person breaches these boundaries. To summarize, physical intimacy between people occurs in the following instances:

1. When people are in each other's physical proximity or private space.
2. When the duration of touch or eye contact exceeds that which is allowed to everyone else.
3. When the level of access to one's body exceeds that which is allowed to everyone else.

Emotional intimacy works in the same way; everything that has been discussed regarding physical intimacy also applies to emotional intimacy.

First, emotional intimacy occurs when someone is allowed into another's private emotional space. When people discuss deeper emotions than what they usually discuss in general with others, they are emotionally intimate. The depth of the emotions being discussed determines the depth of their intimacy. Certain topics are considered private. When these reserved or private topics are discussed with someone, that person is being allowed into one's private emotional space. Proximity to one's pain, joy, and other emotions is emotional intimacy. The closer someone is allowed to private feelings the more intimacy is allowed.

Second, the length of emotional interaction determines the level of emotional intimacy. It is one thing for a co-worker to ask how you are coping after the death of your grandmother. It is emotional intimacy to discuss those feelings longer than simply showing interest and the fact that one cares. The longer those emotions are discussed the more intimacy exists. Emotional intimacy is not always of a romantic nature. They become romantic when the emotions and feelings being discussed concern romantic love. When emotionally intimate feelings are being discussed at length with people with whom you have ongoing relationships it is emotional intimacy. When the same discussion is taking place with a stranger, and whom, in all likelihood, you will never see again, for example, someone sitting next to you in an airplane, the rules change somewhat. There is no risk involved in this "relationship" (what are the chances that you will ever see each other again?) and therefore, it is not deemed to be at the same level of emotional intimacy as it would have been, had the conversation been between you and your partner.

Third, emotional intimacy can be measured by the level of emotional access granted to another. Each person has personal feelings hidden from others. These feelings may be about pain experienced during your childhood, about personal struggles you are going through, or any other topic normally hidden from people. These emotions are not discussed with anyone claiming to be a friend. They are reserved for people with whom we share emotional intimacy. When access to these private and deep feelings and thoughts is granted to someone, access is also granted to one's emotional intimacy.

The deepest level of emotional intimacy is when no emotion is held back and all access is given. Emotional intimacy is the key that unlocks access to deeper emotions to which others (outsiders) usually do not have access. It not only allows the person with whom we are emotionally intimate to interact on a personal level, but to communicate for a longer time than would have been granted to outsiders. If two people do not share emotional intimacy they may tolerate some discussion on a personal level for a short while; but when the discussion gets too intimate or continues for too long we often hear the words, "Now you are getting personal," or "Mind your own business," etc. These are statements telling others to back off; they are too close and an emotional intimate boundary is being crossed without permission. If someone does not back off after being requested to do so, one's emotional intimacy is being violated and it is inappropriate.

Between spouses there should be very few emotional intimate boundaries, if any. There are rare cases, however, where a spouse has been abused or suffered some terrible tragedy in the past, which he or she might not wish to talk about. With the appropriate level of emotional intimacy in place a spouse may seek to peel off the protective layers, exposing the deeper emotions of the partner. Usually a spouse wishes his or her partner to share everything as he or she also wishes to share all. A spouse usually wishes to "uncover" and discover everything of the intimate partner. This, however, is not a one-sided process; As one spouse lets the other into his or her private emotional space, the partner has to reciprocate if intimacy is to last. To enhance emotional intimacy couples, nervously, love to spend time in each other's personal emotional intimate space. "Nervously", as it involves risk; "more time", because it is exhilarating with one another; and spending time being "emotionally intimate" is satisfying to penetrate deeply into each other's space. Couples who enjoy a lot of emotional intimacy are couples that often grant unlimited access to each other's emotional intimate space.

Here, however, lies the problem; many spouses have something hidden, somewhere deep inside, which they do not wish to have uncovered or to be discovered. For someone that may be a "skeleton in the closet." Others may have shared all known "skeletons" already, but they may still have private thoughts and feelings they cling to. They may think that exposing these private issues might dampen emotional intimacy. Some even think that if their spouses know their secret thoughts and issues, they might not be good in their estimation, or that they might be less loved. Many people secretly might wish to ask; "if you knew this or that about me, would you still love me?" Or, "if you really knew who I really am inside, or what I really think, would you still love me?" Most often these questions will not be asked directly because once asked, the secret would be out and the risk would have been taken. When this question is posed it will be too late. We cannot withdraw the question in a way that the spouse will no longer know what the secret is, after hearing an unfavorable answer. The problem with disclosing these hidden and profound feelings is that it involves great risk. It is legitimate to wonder whether I will still be loved if this or that was known. Would such knowledge ruin our relationship, because, after all, substantial issues are at stake? These are challenging questions and no one has guaranteed answers. Yes, there is always a risk in sharing how a person really feels deep down inside. If there was no risk we would share it with everyone.

A spouse, however, is not all and sundry. The boundaries around emotional intimacy are surely a great deal narrower for a spouse than for everyone else. In fact, we have different boundaries, set at different places for every relationship in which we are involved. A spouse is supposed to be privileged with the closest or nearest bounda-ries of all people. It may be true that sharing the deepest hidden secrets could cause problems in relationships. The burden may be too heavy to bear and a spouse may no longer wish to bear it. A spouse may choose not to love you anymore. If these emotions are not shared, however, there will be little emotional intimacy, as that is what emotional intimacy is all about. Remember that the motivating factor for taking any risk is usually some reward. By not taking the risk you forfeit the potential reward (great fulfilling, happy, healthy emotionally intimate relation-ships).

The level of emotional intimacy shared between two people cannot be greater than where the emotional intimacy boundary is set. The wider or further out the boundary is set, the more distant the emotional relationship will be. A boundary is there to protect, by its very design, and it is meant to keep people out. But think about it, all red lights go on if protection is needed from a spouse; in that case, there are greater issues to worry about than emotional intimacy. Happy and healthy intimate relationships (as marriage is supposed to be) should not need boundaries relating to emotional intimacy. Boundaries are intended to keep people out whom we want to keep out (surely we do not want to keep our spouses out). New relationships require broader boundaries as we are not willing to assume huge risks on new comers. As this new relationship develops and deepens these boundaries are rearranged and reset more closely, allowing more access. The placement of this boundary is directly proportional to the level of emotional intimacy enjoyed. If a spouse seeks more emotional intimacy, closer or narrower boundaries have to be set for the partner with whom emotional intimacy is sought.

Since there is risk involved in setting closer boundaries, one does not wish to let go of all the boundaries in a careless way; we do not want to forfeit all the protection that boundaries provide. There are some things, however, that can be done to minimize risk:

First, it is wise to share only feelings whose depth equals the emotional intimacy depth of the relationship. As mentioned in the previous chapter, honesty is always desired. The truth will always come out in the long run; and the sooner it comes out, the less pain there will be. We are not only talking about events and potential skeletons here we are also talking about sharing, opening up to each other. It is advisable, therefore, to share secrets only at an appropriate level of the relationship. The marriage relationship should have already reached the level where sharing everything would be appropriate. An ideal marriage would not have secrets withheld from each other. This does not mean that people will run out of feelings, sensations, sentiments and profound thoughts to share. As long as we are alive and experience events and relationships we will always have new sentiments, thoughts and emotions to share.

Second, it is a good policy to only share feelings and sentiments in depth that are being reciprocated. It would be foolish to assume all the risk. The partner also needs to take the risk of sharing deeper sentiments and feelings. It does not make sense for a person to have a narrow boundary set while the partner maintains a wide boundary. When risk-taking is not balanced between the two people involved, often there is a reason for it; usually that reason spells trouble for the relationship. More about this topic will be discussed later.

Couples were asked about times when they felt close to one another. They were asked to consider when their emotional intimacy had been at its best. We have already seen that the first response was support during a time of crisis. The research also revealed unexpected second responses; all the couples mentioned that conversation enhanced their emotional intimacy in a significant way. So what was different between these conversations and other discussions, which did not make such a positive impact on emotional intimacy? All of these conversations had a number of factors in common:

1. The conversations were all reported by the women.
2. The men were always guiding the conversation.
3. All the men experienced tremendous risk in sharing what they had done or what they felt.
4. Men had no idea that these conversations would build up their wives' emotional intimacy towards them.
5. All of these conversations were about the husbands feeling like failures. They all made themselves vulnerable.

The unexpected gift to emotional intimacy was the exposure of that which was expected to "kill the spark." All the women interviewed stated that when their husbands made themselves vulnerable and shared that which they thought would "kill the fire", they grew much closer to their husbands. When the wives exposed their feelings in these stories many husbands looked on with surprise and amazement. Their original conversations were obviously not planned to be some scheme to trick their wives into greater emotional intimacy. The men simply took the risk; they opened up and allowed their wives into the privacy of their hearts. They allowed their wives into their lives where no one else was allowed to go. Sharing these "secrets" paid huge dividends. We have already seen why women would value it.

These men narrowed their boundaries and let their wives closer into their personal lives. They were willing to find out if they would still be loved once they declared themselves "failures." They shared those aspects that were supposed to be unattractive and repelling. Yet, in so doing they presented their wives with an unexpected gift; the gift of deeper emotional intimacy. That which was supposed to be unattractive and repelling became a magnet. That which was supposed to be a bust for their emotional intimacy turned out to be a boon.

Mike and Jenifer were extremely happily married. Both of them rated their marriage a perfect ten. Both of them said that their emotional intimacy has kept on growing and increasing over the years. When asked what fueled this growth in emotional intimacy over such a long time Jenifer provided the following example:

Mike proposed to her at nineteen, but they did not get married until twenty-one. They were poor at first and lived with Jenifer's parents for a few years to make ends meet. As Jenifer spoke, Mike interjected remarks to explain himself, when he thought it was necessary. During one of these interjections he described himself as a person who always needed a plan. At that stage he was still figuring out his plan, which was a man's way of saying that he did not have one yet. Figuring out a plan, however, did not produce an income as work would. Before long, he remarked, he felt like a failure. He had married Jenifer but he could not take care of her. Her parents had to sustain them. He was not working and was struggling to find work. Mike felt that he was not "being a man." How could he go to Jenifer, however, and tell her that she married "a loser" with no job and no plan of action in place to get one? He thought that telling her how he felt would destroy the emotional intimacy between them. What would she think of him? What would her parents think of him? He thought that telling her would cause her to think of him what he thought of himself, a failure. What could he possibly gain by telling her? He did not know that the unexpected gift to emotional intimacy is the exposure of that which he thought would "kill the fire."

He did not share what persuaded him to disclose this to Jenifer. One day he sat her down and told her what was going on in his mind. He shared how he felt like a failure, how he experienced not "being a man." He really opened himself up to her and provided her with "a no access barred" view of his life, his inner feelings. He shared with her what he has never shared with anyone else. Perhaps he was going through a crisis, but her eyes sparkled as she expressed how his vulnerability enhanced her emotional intimacy towards him. He thought that telling her that he felt like a failure would "kill the fire", but instead this was the unexpected gift to emotional intimacy; the gift that nurtured and grew emotional intimacy. She described this as one of the best events ever that drew them closer together. Looking back Mike agreed that they really felt bonded during and after that discussion. He seemed surprised. It was as if he had only now figured out what the bonding glue was - vulnerability.

John and Betty reported a similar experience. Betty told her story as an example of how and when their fire of emotional intimacy burned most brightly. John was a naval aviator and his training kept him away from home for long periods of time. Eventually he was deployed and he was gone even longer. When he came back and saw that his children had learned new skills, had grown out of their clothing and heard them talking about all their achievements, which he had missed, he felt like an inadequate father. He felt that he was not supportive of the children since he was not able to attend their performances, games, and special events such as birthdays. As he mulled over these thoughts in his mind his negativity grew. He realized that his inadequacy was not only true for his children but also for his wife. Now he felt that he was not only an inadequate father, but also a bad husband. He felt a failure in every aspect of his life.

Eventually he scraped together all the courage he could muster and told her how miserable he was. Would she agree with him and terminate the relationship? Would she add to his burden by telling him how hard things were for her when he was gone? Would she cause him to experience even more pain by disclosing how the children longed for him when he was not there? He never knew that genuine vulnerability was an unexpected gift to emotional intimacy. He did not expect his disclosure to make Betty fall in love with him even deeper. He expected their relationship to fall apart but instead they fell more in love.

She did not think that he was a failure at all. In fact, prior to their marriage, his commitment and sacrifice to the navy made her realize that he would probably also be very committed to her. She knew that not only were they great friends, but also that John would look after himself to come back to her. When Betty heard that John felt like a failure, she appreciated his sacrifices even more. She did not see his failure; she saw his sacrifice for our country. She felt very close to him, even proud of him; their emotional intimacy received a gift. Hearing how he felt about life and what he was thinking helped her to understand him better. She said that it was his vulnerability that drew her closer to him. The fact that he identified the problem and shared it with her without having the solution or being able to fix it enhanced her emotional intimacy with him even more.

He thought that disclosing to her that he felt like a failed father and worthless husband would cause worry; and worry and stress usually dampen intimacy. Women typically think, however, that non-disclosure is a symptom of a dwindling fire (punishment by exclusion). Men usually think that exposing their intimate thoughts would kill the fire, but actually it would fuel the fire. As John and Betty discussed the issue and their future, they felt their emotional intimacy enhanced.

Although it does not make sense to men, exposure of secrets pertaining to weakness and vulnerability fuels the fire of emotional intimacy. Women long for the day when men would take the risk and provide the gift of opening up, eradicating "Mr. Tough-guy", and becoming vulnerable. No, women do not interpret this as weakness; and no, there is no competition between a husband and his wife on this score. Men do not have to project an image of strength, and there is no enemy that needs to be conquered; it is simply he and she alone. She interprets the sharing of secrets as closeness. She interprets the lack of sharing as punishment by exclusion. Not sharing male vulnerability robs her of emotional intimacy. Sharing male vulnerability enriches emotional intimacy; whether this is unexpected or not.

Women would benefit by realizing that men only feel a need to share that which they cannot fix themselves with the person they believe who may have the solution. If he thinks she cannot fix it, he sees no reason to share it with her. For a husband, focused on solutions and fixing things, there is no point in sharing an issue with his wife if she cannot do anything about it. Men are oriented to solutions and a fix-it-attitude, and not to a networking- and bonding-orientation. Not sharing secrets is not a weapon in men's armory to punish wives; in fact, it never even crosses their minds. After all, have you ever heard a man say; "now I am not going to be physically intimate with you tonight because you did ... or did not ...?"

It does not come easily to men to share vulnerability. It flies in the face of the accepted social definition of "being a man"; it goes against everything they know, and it is the same as admitting defeat. Women can assist men to share more by creating an environment where it is safe for them to take risks. No, nagging does not do the job. Men can be helped to share their vulnerability by being persuaded that they are on the same team "competing" against the problem and not against each other.

Men do not always make sense to women. Women are not always comprehensible to men; in fact, they almost never are. We do not even always understand ourselves, how are we to understand someone else fully? Fortunately, understanding each other is not required for great emotional intimacy. Simply exploring each other together achieves greater emotional intimacy. Exploring each other in areas of vulnerability fans the flames of emotional intimacy.

Men see male vulnerability as a "flaw." Women view that same vulnerability, when shared, as a gift to emotional intimacy. To her it does not really matter how men view vulnerability, does it? So why let the male view of vulnerability dictates whether issues are shared or not? As far as women are concerned, only what women think about male vulnerability matters. It is hardly relevant to her that he thinks sharing vulnerability is a sign of weakness. It is more relevant for him to know that she loves him making himself vulnerable to her.

Women and men are certainly different and we find it difficult to understand each other. We are not called, however, to understand each other; we are called to love each other. We are called to make ourselves "vulnerable." We are called to expose to each other that which no one else is allowed to see. Sharing and accessing intimate feelings and thoughts generates emotional intimacy, especially for women.

Tom had had some problems long before he met Jane. He was a drinker and used drugs; when this interview took place Tom had been "clean" and sober for about six years. He was asked to share a story relating to the time when he and Jane felt closest to one another. At first the selection of this particular story as an example of great emotional intimacy made no sense, as it indicated the opposite. It would never have made sense was it not for the very last part; making one vulnerable to one's wife seems to perform miracles with regard to emotional intimacy.

Tom, Jane and her mother and stepfather, drove from California to the East Coast to purchase a boat and to bring it back to California. The boat was half price and they thought that it was worth the effort and traveling expense. Everything went well traveling to the East Coast and they bought the boat. It was on the way back that tragedy struck. They had reached Nashville and decided to stay overnight. Being thirsty from driving all day long, Tom decided that he needed a drink (yes, the kind of drink he should have rather avoided). Unfortunately, it did not stay with just one drink. Neither he, nor Jane said what happened that night other than to mention that Tom was embarrassed. The next day they continued their journey to California; the remainder of the previous night's argument continued as well. Halfway back from Nashville, they received a call informing them that Jane's biological father had just passed away. Since they were relatively close to where her father used to live, Tom decided to drive the extra way to attend the funeral. This decision to go to the funeral, however, caused a disagreement between Tom and his mother-in-law. The disagreement continued until they stopped for gas. Tom was in trouble with Jane for the previous night's embarrassment and the ensuing arguments and now he was also in trouble with his mother-in-law.

The next thing Tom knew Jane gave him enough money for a bus ticket to California, dropped him off at Greyhound, and drove off without him. At least Tom was not stuck in Texas. After two days on the Greyhound bus he made it home. Then he changed jobs and started with his new work. Tom did not mention where he lived during the next month. What he said was that it took him more than a month before he could see Jane again; and this story was supposed to be about great emotional intimacy? One day, however, close to the end of work, she came to his new job to see him. They went down to the beach and started walking hand in hand; they just walked and walked, and they just talked and talked. As they spoke he became more genuine; he made himself vulnerable and admitted his problems and acknowledged his mistakes. He shared with her how he struggled with drinking and drugs; the very thing she warned him about. Tom, however, said he was sorry and asked Jane to forgive him.

Admitting guilt and admitting sorrow are difficult for men to do because it is like admitting defeat and losing to the "competition." Perhaps she would become annoyed with him for still being involved with these substances after she ruled this out for him. Perhaps she would see him as a loser and leave him for good this time. What if she got him another Greyhound ticket, this time back to Texas? She did not, however. She enjoyed being led into the profoundest depths of his heart, his struggles, and his failures. They walked so far that they got tired and they just lay down on the beach to take a nap. Jane said of that nap; "it was so pleasant to be together, to be on the beach and to listen to the ocean; and we got back together." It appeared as if Tom's willingness to make him vulnerable and to open himself up to Jane really and truly saved his marriage. It is now many years later and they are still together.

The emotional intimacy between them was so deep and profound during that beach walk and their talk, that to this day, Tom thought of this story as an example of feeling close to Jane; a story which most of us would rather have chosen to forget.

When men share their vulnerability they become genuine; their shields and masks come off. Total access to these most private thoughts is the ultimate gift to emotional intimacy that can be given; this is the kind of intimacy women dream of. The fact of the matter is that other men might think more of him because of all his victories and achievements, but a woman would think more of him for letting her in to where no one else could go. Sex is not quite possible with clothes on; likewise, one cannot be emotionally intimate with covered feelings, with hidden thoughts and with veiled sensitivities buried in some chamber deep within the heart where no one else can access it. Using our own methods to evaluate ourselves is only valid for us. If we wish to know what other people think of us, we have to use as a gauge that which they would use to measure us with. That gauge for women is how willing men are to open up to them; how far a man is willing to let her in, and for how long she is allowed to stay close. Those who have taken the risk have reaped the reward. It might just be that when we open up and make ourselves vulnerable we are also opening up an unexpected gift; deeper emotional intimacy.

Honesty demands a word of caution here. Exposure of vulnerability has to be genuine to be fostering real emotional intimacy. A person cannot be a failure without any genuine intention to change and still expect to be applauded just because that person shared issues and brought them into the open, the openness within their marriage.

Furthermore, repeated failures leave deep wounds. Making known the vulnerability that underlies them does not magically heal those wounds. A long process of healing may be ahead. That process of healing goes hand in hand with the process of correcting the mistakes. No correction - no healing. Some relationships might be so damaged that healing requires a "miracle." Miracles would not be called miracles if they happened in abundance. It is not wise to be foolish in order to create an opportunity whereby a person has something to be vulnerable about.

In addition, revealing what is hidden might cause hurt and consequently, will not be seen as a gift bringing emotional intimacy. In fact, emotional intimacy can land in the trash, gift wrapper and all. Many a man has had flowers tossed back into his face. If a wounding history is damaging, damage may still be caused. Honesty is still the best policy. I do not want to create a false hope that by telling your spouse of your failure all the hurt will disappear and somehow he or she is going to be mesmerized by you. Telling a spouse all about it, by itself, may not undo the damage. At least telling one's spouse now will not make it worse than if it is found out later; quite the contrary. Emotional intimacy "floating" on lies will eventually burst open. The kind of vulnerability that is a gift to emotional intimacy is when we share deep feelings and thought about what we are going through; not about something terrible we did.

False emotional intimacy is actually not emotional intimacy at all. Fabricated emotional intimacy is like taking one's spouse within the boundary of privacy, allowing the spouse to enter, but to thoughts, feelings, sentiments and events that do not portray the real picture. When the spouse discovers a false portrayal there will be no one trustworthy to come back to for healing, comfort, and the rebuilding of a relationship.

If we are honest and doing our best, but we still make a mistake in the process, and we tell our partner about it, there will at least be a real person to come back to. A relationship can always be rebuilt. A phony person can only rebuild a phony relationship.

May I challenge you to be real and genuine with your spouse? Please consider making yourself vulnerable and letting your spouse in. Vulnerability is the unexpected gift to emotional intimacy which helps to create surefire romantic relationships.

∂ CHAPTER SEVEN ∂

"TO KNOW" OR "NOT TO KNOW?"

We have already seen that women's relationships are all about networking, connecting, and bonding. When these take place their relationships flourish. On the other hand, we explored the concept of "punishment" by "exclusion" for women. Whether men intent to brush off their wives by way of "exclusion" or not, this is interpreted as being shunned. Most men may not know this; as a result they have no idea why their wives feel distant from them. Many men, confronted with a divorce, are completely surprised and shocked as they had no idea that anything was wrong. As far as they were concerned the emotional intimacy between them was just great; but their wives felt alone and isolated because of a lack of continuous connection and bonding. In general, men seem to consider connecting and bonding mostly in physical terms. Women regard their connecting and bonding in terms of sharing innermost thoughts and feelings; they need to know what is going on and they need to ascertain the details of what is happening in their husband's lives. For men, on the other hand, it is all about the big picture, the bottom line, the main issue and the outcome.

Just think back about the last time you and your partner enjoyed a movie together. The next evening you two visited some friends. You told them about watching the movie the previous night and they enquired about the movie. If the husband is telling the story, he will describe the plot in approximately a minute. If asked about the characters of the movie, he could also describe the main characters in a few moments. Should he wish to disclose more information he would typically describe "action" or "objects", for example, an airplane or a fancy car used in the movie. Perhaps he would include the special effects or the location of the story as part of the conversation. If the wife told the story, however, she would describe the plot of the movie in details, perhaps taking as long as the movie lasted. She would go into all the particulars, what they said, what they did, how they felt, and so forth. She would not need to be asked about the characters, because for her it would be all about the relationships between the characters, and she would automatically speak about the characters. Her description would be more people-based and she would focus on the relationships. Men perceive and appreciate the big picture; women understand and value the intricate details of the relationships.

So, conversations in marriage typically follow the same pattern of him talking about the comprehensive picture and her wishing to disclose the details. As she might be telling him about all the details, he would be wondering when she would get to the point and what the point might be. Men often wonder why women tell their stories to begin with, as they feel that there is no point to their detailed stories. Usually she has lots to say, he does not. What is important is that the husband should realize when she talks about all the details it is an attempt to connect with him. When he does not talk about all the particulars she thinks that he does not make an effort to connect, therefore, according to her, he does not wish to connect with her or he excludes her. She feels "punished" by exclusion and cannot understand what she has done wrong to deserve this punishment. What makes matters even worse is that men are unaware that they punish their wives by so-called exclusion. It just happens automatically because men are not interested in the relational details of other people; they believe it's all about the big picture, and that is all they share. When women enthusiastically tell their husbands all about their day, the husbands do not listen to all the details, as they find that irrelevant; they only listen to hear the big picture, the one minute summary. While she tells the story she notices that he is not "listening."

While it is true that he is not listening the way women do, and also that he is not showing interest in all the details, he is actually listening carefully, but he is only listening to obtain the big picture. The purpose of ascertaining facts, for men, is only to identify problems and solve them. She wants to know about and understand issues, aiming towards connecting and bonding. Since bonding and connecting is what relationships are all about for women, and as knowing creates bonding and connecting, women simply have to know the details. Women listen to comprehend and form networks; men listen to identify the problems. If there is no problem, there is no need to listen other than to have a good time. Likewise, a man does not see the logic in telling his wife something that does not concern some logistics or problems; unless of course he is the main character of the story; and if he is not the main character the story may very well be about how unfair the main character has treated him.

If a conversation takes place in a crowded room with a lot of noise and many conversations going on all over the place, usually a man is still able to hear when someone mentions his name, even though he talks to someone else and is not concentrating or attempting to hear what others say. This is called "selective attention." This is really how men hear or listen. Women's conversations are like background noise for men, like unfamiliar people's conversations. When women voice a problem this is for men a synonym or alternative for "competition"; their ears perk up and they pick it up. Without mentioning a problem, however, they simply hear "meaningless" discussion, of only entertainment value. The conversation is heard, but no attention is paid to it, and no response is warranted.

Consequently, it is no surprise that one of the main complaints of women about relationships with their men is that they do not feel acknowledged and understood. "Men hear, but they do not listen". If a man assumed that he understood the "big picture" and he provided a solution, she would not feel acknowledged and understood at all. She would not feel acknowledged, as she told the story intending to be listened to, to connect and build relationships, not to find solutions. By offering solutions the man, without knowing it, would convey to her that he totally missed the point with regard to "connecting" with her, as the discussion was simply not about a problem; it was about relationships. A man is simply not good at determining whether his wife tells him something to bond or whether she wants him to assist.

Men tell other men stories and convey information about their lives to compete and also to impress them, to entertain, or to find solutions. Men do not seem to understand that women talk to bond. While she tells him a story his mind is working overtime to figure out whether she is competing, and with whom, or whether she needs a solution. If she tells him what a bad day she has had, he wants to know what or who has made it such a bad day. If he found that her boss was the cause of her bad day he would assume that she and her boss were "competing." He would proceed by providing her advice on how to triumph in this rivalry. She, however, did not wish to win a contest; she simply desired to "connect." Her desire to connect can be so strong that she would accept bad days as the price to pay to eventually establish a connection and to obtain collaboration with her boss, which would be worth her while. When it ends up that she did not tell him the story to compete or to find a solution, the man wonders what possibly could have motivated her to tell the story in the first place. He would be uncertain how to react.

When women tell men that men do not listen or care, men are often perplexed because they feel that offering solutions and fixing things offers support and demonstrates caring. Tendering support for men is what enhances emotional intimacy. Women feel shunned when "excluded", and men feel rejected when their advice or solutions are "disregarded." Men take these things personally; they do not think that their wives would not like the idea, but they feel rejected as a person. As women feel that men "hear, but do not listen", men feel disregarded when their "solutions and advice are not accepted." Both men and women communicate inadvertently past each other and both get hurt in the process. Consequently, emotional intimacy ends up in the trashcan.

Do you remember how men will lie in order to protect their wives from "pain"? Do you remember that men use what they consider an effective method to protect their wives from "pain", namely not to tell her about issues? We have also seen that men are not very good at hiding the fact that they struggle with something. Women just know, however, that something is going on in their men's lives. Women just know when men are quieter than usual. It seems to women, and correctly so, that men are distant or distracted when dealing with problems, they appear to be buried deeply in their thoughts. Women can detect that they are worried and experiencing discomfort. When women experience that something is wrong they simply have to know the details; knowing and sharing connect them to each other.

When a woman notices that something is happening in her husband's life she rejoices, not because something, probably something bad, is happening with him, but because she detects a golden opportunity to bond and to connect. This means that he has a secret they can share and their emotional intimacy is about to grow, and what can be better for them? Unfortunately, he does not see it that way, as we have seen in the previous chapter. He does not wish to burden her with his problems and struggles. He thinks that he is doing the "manly thing;" to bear the burden and to protect her from its load. That, however, is not true for her; he is not protecting her; the moment she knows that something is going on in his life she also has a burden and wishes to know what it is. That burden, "not to know", is often a larger burden to her than for him to "know" his problem.

Emotional intimacy is partially measured by women by the depth and frequency of the secrets shared. When women detect that there is something going on in their husbands' lives it seems to them that it is usually something severe and serious; this presents the perfect opportunity to connect and bond. After all, there has to be a secret to be shared, the more important and secretive the better. They just have to know what the issue is. As much as she wishes to know, he wishes to protect her from knowing and, consequently, not to suffer "pain."

The more he attempts to hide the matter the more it convinces her that there must be an intimate and deep secret. This makes the "secret" more desirable as it will create more and deeper bonding. She begins to pursue the issue, and he feels pressed and withdraws. In turn, his withdrawal makes her feel rejected and shunned. Consequently, she pursues it more intensely. A vicious cycle might develop, detrimental to both of them. Neither of them would understand the other's actions. Both of them would interpret the other's actions from their own specific point of view, which is gender-oriented. This interpretation is typically not good news and cools off emotional intimacy.

Reinterpreting each other's actions from the other's point of view, which is gender-oriented, brings understanding and compassion. It changes their behavior, but it is not easy and it does not happen overnight, nevertheless emotional intimacy increases.

This is rather a difficult obstacle to overcome, as a woman's feelings of being excluded run deep and it hurts; in fact, it shatters her emotional intimacy. On the other hand, a man does not feel that he is doing what a man is supposed to do if he allows her to share the "pain." He feels like a failure if he does not protect her successfully. A battle now ensues; she wishes to know what is going on while he does not wish her to "know" it. Women cannot understand why he does not want her to "know", for knowing is connecting. Men cannot understand why women wish to know, for "knowing" is "pain." Both of them battle with the question, "to know" or "not to know." She opts for knowing; he opts for her not to know.

They now employ opposite tactics to achieve their goals; she, on the one hand, just knows that something is going on with him. So, as an icebreaker she asks him what is wrong, or why he is so quiet. This question is an invitation to talk and to connect; but that question, on the other hand, also poses a threat to his need of not letting her "know" what is going on. Consequently, he either avoids answering the question or withdraws. She does not understand that he wishes to protect her. He does not understand that not letting her "know" goes against everything she knows about connecting and bonding. As her questions about what is going on do not produce results, she tries harder and continuously. Before long she is prying, asking and nagging, using every opportunity she gets. The more she does this, the more he withdraws and avoids the issue. The more he withdraws and avoids the issue the more she feels excluded, so, she tries harder and more often. This establishes a cycle of draining each other's emotional intimacy and ruins it. A woman may see nagging as an icebreaker to talk and to connect, but in actual fact nagging just alienates her husband.

Men might not know what enhances their emotional intimacy, but women know what enriches theirs. Men, however, know for sure what drains their emotional intimacy; *the primary factor is not feeling supported by their wives.* The secondary draining is prying, continuous questioning, criticism and nagging. So, when a woman nags to retrieve her husband's "secrets" to bond more with him she is unknowingly ruining his emotional intimacy even though she may think otherwise. The problem is that if she does not find out what is going on with her husband her emotional intimacy gets drained. Consequently, she feels that she has to "know" at all costs. He feels that he has to protect her from knowing at all costs; so, we have to ask the important question, "to know" or "not to know"?

The research on this issue found that wives wish their husbands would learn to share their issues. Men wish their wives would stop nagging. Men view nagging as disruptive to peace and they just wish to have peace at home. Their whole lives are filled with "competition." At home they do not want to continue that struggle; here they need someone on their side, someone to extend support. Peace, to men, often means simply to drop a matter, instead of hammering on it all the time.

James told a story about his youth. He often went out to the field where his grandpa was working. Then they sat under a tree while his grandpa ate an apple or some fruit and told him some stories; he often repeated one of these stories. As James grew older and got married he always remembered the final conclusion of that repeated story; James looked up into the air as if he still saw his grandpa sitting at the tree. A smile of remembrance appeared on his face as he quoted his grandpa's conclusion; "when mamma is happy, the house is happy and everyone is happy." That is what men wish to have.

The problem for women is that "mamma cannot not be happy when papa is not happy." Women seem to have a sixth sense to know when "papa is not happy." The only thing that would make mamma happy is when papa discloses what is bothering him. A woman has an intense desire to find out what is bothering him. This means that she is not interfering in his business, but that she simply wishes to connect with him. Her emotional intimacy seems to perish if there is such a thing as "his business" in the marriage relationship. A woman sees everything relational, as "our business", because she and her husband are connected. The stronger the connection the more emotional intimacy for her and a lack of connectedness means a lack of emotional intimacy. This is a simple open and shut case.

If a man and a woman wish to resolve the battle between "knowing" and "not knowing", and if they wish to have peace, happiness and intimacy, a realignment of their thinking needs to take place. Men reported that they wish their wives would learn to wait until they were ready to share their issues, or to find another way to find out what was going on that did not involve nagging. Nagging was reported simply to add extra weight to the husband's heavy burdens. Now, he has to worry not only about the burden, but he also has to worry about keeping her from "knowing" the issues, which he equates with "pain" for her.

Women reported that men's refusal to open up "hurts" and confuses them. If men wish to get wives on their side and supporting them, wives "need to know the issue" to be able to support them. Women often wonder, "are we a team or not?" If we were a team, then sharing these things would be a necessity. If we were not a team, there could be no emotional intimacy.

The husband and wife just listen differently and for differently things; they just share differently and also share different things. We would be well advised to understand these differences and it would make such a difference if we knew the "pain" and disadvantages these differences cause. If we could place ourselves only into each other's shoes, or rather, mindsets; emotional intimacy is all about truly knowing each other and each other's struggles.

A husband could be equated to a vault with regard to sharing struggles and worries; if the vault is locked up, the secret will be safe, but at the same time his wife is locked out. The value of a vault is to keep something safe inside and simultaneously to keep others out. Keeping these secrets safe, however, comes at a price; excluding his wife. It is not possible to lock the safe without ruining their emotional intimacy at the same time. An open vault leads to a "safer" and more satisfying relationship.

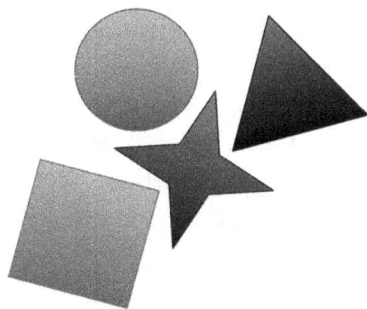

❧ CHAPTER EIGHT ❧

TEMPERAMENTS AND EMOTIONAL INTIMACY

There are usually at least four types of temperaments: The ancient Greek philosophers called the four of them Phlegmatic, Choleric, Melancholy and Sanguine. Many different forms of tests are employed to evaluate and classify temperament types, using different names for each temperament - that, however, is a topic for another day. Temperaments and personality types are complex subjects and may require highly trained people to interpret them. We are not concerned with all the complex models used to discuss temperaments for our purposes here. With your kind permission we will simplify the matter to enable us to describe how a basic understanding of temperaments influences emotional intimacy.

Temperaments can be described by using two lines, one vertical and one horizontal, crossing one another. The horizontal line, from the left to the right, represents how reserved or outgoing a person is. On the far left of this line we find a person who is very introverted and private. On the far right of this line is a person who is very outgoing. Approximately 50% of all people are on the one side of the line and approximately 50% on the other side. The vertical line, from top to bottom, represents how "emotional" or "unemotional" we are, or better, how much emotion a person displays, or how little, as all people are emotion.

Another way to look at this is to think of "emotional" people as people-oriented and "unemotional" people as task-oriented. This does not mean that "unemotional" people do not have emotions; it simply means that they do not show or display their emotions so easily and that emotions do not play as big a part in their decision-making process as those who are "emotional", or showing more emotion. Approximately half of all people are "emotional" people and the other half are "unemotional." If these two lines intersect to form two axes of a graph, four quadrants are created. These four quadrants are combinations of each line's attributes. Each combination constitutes a different temperament and, thus, we have four temperaments:

- A Phlegmatic person is someone who is introverted and "unemotional."
- A Choleric person is extroverted and "unemotional."
- A Melancholy person is introverted and "emotional."
- Lastly, a Sanguine person is both extroverted and "emotional."

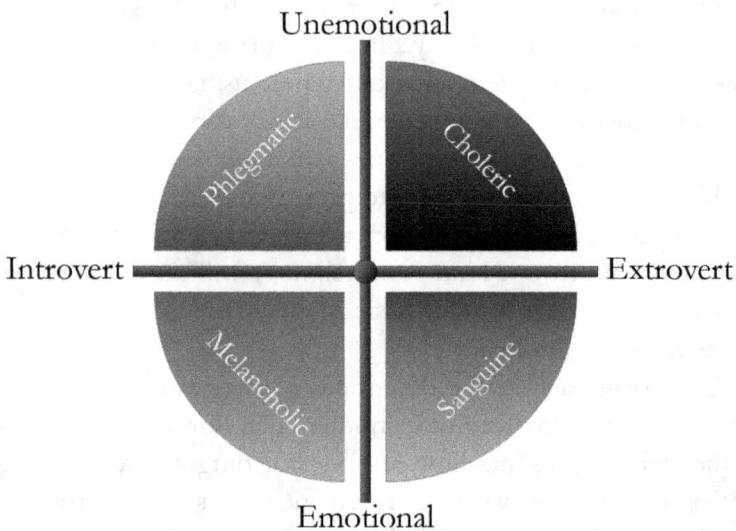

A person's position on these lines determines how strong the traits are. Someone on the right edge of the extrovert line is a great deal more outgoing than someone who is barely over the middle of the line on the extroverted side. The same is true for a person's position on the vertical line. People tend to "mellow" out to some extent as they mature (senior citizens may intensify again toward the end of life) and they can learn to be more outgoing or to show less emotion, for example, but our natural position on the diagram does not change a lot after adulthood. When we are with people we know well and are comfortable with, we tend to move slightly to the right, becoming more extroverted, and we also move to the bottom, showing more emotion. Conversely, when we are with people we do not know well and are not comfortable with, we move slightly to the left, and become more reserved, and we also move to the top, showing less emotion.

Four people drive in a car into a mall's parking area; as they turn into the parking space they see a beggar with a sign, asking for money:

- Mr. Melancholic looks at the beggar and thinks: "Poor beggar, he looks hungry and he probably had no bath for a week. Although Mr. Melancholic thinks about the situation he does not say anything. He dwells on this person's plight for some time and thinks about his own tough times in the past.

- Mrs. Sanguine sees the beggar and immediately starts voicing her feelings to everyone in the car: "Look," she says, "that beggar's clothing is all torn and he is scorched by the sun, standing there for many long hours. The poor guy does not even have a place to sit down; just imagine standing in the sun all day long without any rest. Let's help him."

- Mrs. Phlegmatic listens to Mrs. Sanguine and starts analyzing the situation. She observes everything and notices that the beggar's car is parked just to his left. She knows that it is his car because of the way it is packed and because of its contents. She thinks: "Perhaps this guy is not as poor as he pretends to be, as that is not a bad-looking car."

- Mrs. Phlegmatic also notices that Mr. Beggar is smoking and she argues as follows silently in her mind: "If he has money to pay for expensive cigarettes to burn up then he should also have money for food. If he does not have money for food it is his own fault since he wastes it on non-essentials, like cigarettes. I will not help him as I will not subsidize his smoking habit." Mrs. Phlegmatic may also not yet say anything to the group at that stage.

- Then Mr. Choleric speaks: "I will not help the beggar since he is simply lazy. I do not believe that it is our duty to sustain a person who does not want to work."
- Mrs. Sanguine replies: "How do you know that he is lazy and do not want to work?"
- Mr. Choleric answers: "Just look at his sign, he is asking for money, not for a job. Furthermore, there are numerous cars in this parking lot and I do not see him asking anyone if he can wash cars for a fee. If a person like that came to me and offered to wash my car for a fee I would support him. I would not support him, however, if he made no effort at all, but simply stood there."
- Mrs. Sanguine and Mr. Choleric may argue for some time. They dominate the discussion.
- Mrs. Sanguine speaks passionately and brings feelings and emotions into play.
- Mr. Choleric uses logic, rational thinking, facts and figures to attack Mrs. Sanguine's position.
- Yet, during all this time neither Mr. Melancholic nor Mrs. Phlegmatic has spoken up. They have been busy analyzing the situation.
- Mr. Melancholic spends some time thinking of the past. Perhaps he had a family member that suffered a similar fate as this beggar.
- Mrs. Phlegmatic observes all she sees. She analyzes the conversation between the two extroverts. The two introverts may only speak after some time. Introverts often speak after others have already made a decision. Yet, they bring valuable food for thought.
- Mr. Melancholic may want to help the beggar while Mrs. Phlegmatic may be less inclined.

The four temperaments are not just referring to having certain traits as it reflects a whole different way of thinking. If we see the same situation, a beggar for example, *our different ways of thinking influences our interpretation of the situation.* Our interpretation of events is what we consider to be the truth. These interpretations shape our action whether we would give the beggar money or not, for example.

Couples often experience the same event, but interpret it totally differently. The differences in interpretation, or seeing things differently, lead to many disagreements between couples, or worse, a great deal of tension. We have already seen how gender differences influence the way we see things. Temperaments are another important influence on the way we interpret or see things, and how we think and act.

Since temperaments affect the way we see things, and how we think and act, it also influences emotional intimacy. It even makes an impact on the way we see each other and interpret what happens between people. In some situations "emotional" people think of "unemotional" persons as "cold and hard", even cruel. At the same time "unemotional" people are tempted to think of "emotional" people as weak and easily manipulated. It is very important, therefore, to know what these differences are and how to treat our spouses if they and we have different temperaments.

At the end of a long day's work a couple arrives home, tired. The introverted person thinks: "Oh good, I am at home at last. I can now relax and 'recharge' by just being quiet and peaceful. Our home is a haven of rest where I can escape from business, from all the talking, and from people." Introverted people are "recharged" or invigorated by taking a break from people. People, and especially too many other people, drain their energy. Introverted people require energy to interact with people, as it does not come as naturally to them as to extroverted people.

The extroverted person thinks: "Oh good, I am home at last. I can now spend some time with my spouse. We can talk and have a good time together. Then after a while perhaps we can go out to visit some friends." Extroverted people are "recharged" by being with people. Being alone and not interacting with others drains their energy. *A quiet place is a dead place as far as extroverted people are concerned, but please remember, a quiet place is a haven for introverted people. This couple's needs are now in conflict with each other.*

The introverted person says that he or she is tired and does not want to go out with friends. The extroverted person says that he or she is tired and, therefore, wishes to be invigorated by interaction with friends. To protect emotional intimacy between you and your spouse it is beneficial to learn that temperaments cause us to think and act differently. It is valuable to understand whether a spouse's "batteries are recharged" or "drained" by people. This understanding and insight can be used to decide whether a calm space and a quiet time are required or whether interaction is required. It is important to accept the fact that we all differ and that we have different needs, which does not mean at all that we do not love each other and that we do not wish to be with one another; it simply means that we are different. *Introverted people often feel overwhelmed and smothered by extroverted people, and extroverted people often feel abandoned and discarded by introverted people.* These feelings can have a very negative impact on our emotional intimacy if we do not understand these differences.

Introverted people do not talk as much as extroverted people and are especially content to be alone. Extroverted people can talk all day long and do not enjoy being alone, at least not for very long. Introverted people analyze everything and take time dealing with opinions and thoughts in their minds; as a result, they need time to make decisions, and feel pressured when they are required to make a quick decision when they are not ready. Extroverted people do not analyze everything so intensely and tend to make decisions quickly. It frustrates extroverted people when others do not seem to make up their minds. They may see introverted people as sluggish and lethargic.

When a couple needs to make a decision it may be good to consider these differences, as a failure to do so will make a negative impact on the emotional intimacy between them. An introverted person needs advance notice of the time when a decision is to be taken; they hate pressure, and they need to be reminded from time to time that a decision is due by a certain date as the deadline draws near. Since they analyze everything it may be wise to ask them periodically if they need more information that would be helpful in their decision-making process. The long decision-making process of introverted people may frustrate an extroverted person. They regard it as indecision. When dealing with an extrovert it may be the best to remind them from time to time that introverted people have not forgotten that a decision is due; they simply process longer than extroverted people.

Extroverted people need to be reassured that there is still enough time left before the due date and that nothing is gained by deciding right away. Introverted people will do well to inform extroverted people that taking time to analyze and process a decision is important to them even though it may not be necessary for extroverted people. When an introverted person needs to make a decision, there seems to be less frustration because typically the decision has already been analyzed before the request for a decision is even made, and the extroverted person will render their decision right away, provided that there is enough information and they have had the information sufficiently in advance to analyze and think about the matter. When an extroverted person provides their answer, Mr. or Mrs. Introvert will save them distress by not questioning the speed at which the answer comes, or the amount of knowledge and information used in the decision-making process. Extroverts and introverts just function and think differently.

There are also differences between those who display more emotion and those who retain or hold back emotion. "Emotional" people laugh out loud or they may cry visibly during a movie. "Unemotional" people also laugh at a movie, but they keep their laughs inside; they are also happy, but they do not feel as though they have to show tears or celebration to demonstrate their happiness. They may be sad, but they may not show it. The main distinction though is that "unemotional" people do not base their decisions so much on their emotions, whereas "emotional" people rely on their emotions, how they experience their sentiments and take decisions. "Unemotional" people mostly make decisions based upon "facts", figures and logic. They are task-oriented, and their work is primary. "Emotional" people are more people-oriented, and people are most important. They are typically interested in people and their stories.

- Mr. "Unemotional" is busy mowing the lawn as the neighbor arrives. The neighbor greets Mr. "Unemotional" and comes closer to talk to him. Mr. "Unemotional" greets the neighbor and then remarks: "I am almost done with the lawn and only have this small portion left. Give me a minute, please, just to finish this, and then I will be with you." He continues finishing mowing the lawn. Mr. "Unemotional" is not rude, he is just task-oriented and his task is at hand.
- Mr. "Emotional" is busy mowing the lawn as the neighbor arrives. The neighbor greets Mr. "Emotional" and comes closer to talk to him. Mr. "Emotional" instantly switches off the lawn

mower and goes over to the neighbor to converse. After all, the lawn can wait - people come first. If Mr. "Emotional" is extroverted he sees in Mr. "Neighbor" an opportunity to take a well-deserved break - an opportunity to "recharge" and to be invigorated. If he is introverted, however, he reasons and thinks that it is the right thing to do; after all, Mr. "Neighbor" has always been kind and helpful to him; and now he is just returning the favor. "Emotional" spouses may regularly hear their "unemotional" spouses say: "Let me just finish this", or "just give me a minute." "Unemotional" spouses may regularly hear their "emotional" spouses say, "This can wait" or "I will do this later." Mr. "Emotional" is not lazy; he is just people-oriented. Mr. "Unemotional" is not unresponsive to people, he is just task-oriented.

- If a decision is to be made, "unemotional" people need to know the facts, figures, and logic to enable them to make a decision. "Emotional" people need to know the humanistic and humane stories behind the decision. They need to know how this decision will impact people.

We tend, however, to think that other people's thinking and behavior work like ours. So, if I want facts, figures and logic to make a decision I assume that my spouse will also automatically need facts, figures and logic to make a decision. If I tell her about the decision, I think that I am doing her a favor by giving her all the facts, figures and logic. If she is not also task-oriented like me, however, those things are not so important to her. She needs to know the story behind the decision, how I feel, and how the decision will impact us for her to make a decision. Similarly, "emotional" people tell long stories about people and their stories behind the decision and how it impacts them when requiring a decision from an "unemotional" person. While this story is being told the "unemotional" person thinks: "Oh, this is just a sob story." If we can supply our spouses with the type of information, factual or humanity-oriented, needed by him or her rather than what we deem to be important, our decision making will be more pleasant. Consequently, our emotional intimacy will not be drained, and misunder-standing and frustration levels will decrease.

To summarize:

- Phlegmatic people are hardworking and loyal. Phlegmatic people need space and time; it is best not to spring surprises on them, and not to request them to make a decision right away. It is helpful to provide them with all the facts, figures and logic and give them a deadline for their decision.
- Melancholic people make excellent friends once they let you in. Melancholy people also need space and time; they do not like surprises or to be asked to make a decision right away. Melancholic people need to hear about the story and the people behind the decision. They need to find out how these situations have been dealt with in the past before they feel comfortable to make their decisions. They also prefer to know the deadline when a decision is needed.
- Choleric people are "driven", motivated and self-disciplined; they wish to make things happen. Facts, figures and logic drive their decision-making process and they are often ready to make a decision right away.
- Sanguine people are "people's people;" they need to hear about the people and their stories behind the decision. As with Choleric people Sanguines tend to take decisions right away.

Learning how to deal with your spouse's temperament will make your spouse more comfortable and feel more respected. The feelings of being pressured or slowed down will decrease.

If both spouses are introverts, they will need more time for processing. Deadlines will have to be communicated clearly, and each spouse needs to know who is responsible for what.

If both spouses are extroverts, there is a danger that a great deal of talking may result in less doing, especially if both are Sanguine. If both spouses are "unemotional", it may be a pleasant surprise and realization that life does not have to be that serious – life can be enjoyed and savored, and people do matter more than perhaps previously thought. If both spouses are "emotional", gullibility may be a problem – there are people out there eager to take advantage of others.

Discussing of each spouse's different temperament type may be very useful and helpful. Understanding who he or she really is and how he or she thinks and views things removes a great deal of frustration and misunderstanding. Couples benefit from discussing steps needed to deal better with him or her in ways that favor his or her personality. Accepting each other's differences rather than wishing to change a spouse has a wonderful influence on emotional intimacy. We would do well to learn how to deal with the different temperaments from the other person's perspective and not our own, as far as possible.

Relationships are all about relating to each other. Temperaments regulate to a large extent how we relate and how we interpret each other's way of relating. We can make our way of relating pleasant, free from unnecessary stress, and respectful by relating in such a way as to what our spouse's temperament prefers.

A great deal of emotional intimacy is lost because of temperament clashes and hostility because we see things differently. Emotional intimacy is negatively affected if we judge a spouse according to our temperament, rather than by his or her temperament. What would be considered "cold" by Mr. Sanguine, relationally and not according to temperature, would not be considered "cold" by Mrs. Phlegmatic. Having the "correct" view, as viewed from the appropriate temperament, is a better basis for a more accurate judgment. We would be a great deal better off if we considered and took each other's temperaments into account more often. The advantages are pronounced for building emotional intimacy and the negative effects are grave if we do not take them into account. Temperaments and emotional intimacy "hold hands" and work together. Sure, emotional intimacy requires an understanding of our spouses' temperament and, therefore, an adaptation to the way we relate.

⟡ CHAPTER NINE ⟡

ROOT CAUSES OF MISFIRE

Our family background played a vital role in shaping who we become. We personally also play an important part ourselves because we choose how to react to what had happens to us. Who we are going to be in future are being shaped every day by life experiences and the choices we make as a result.

A relationship is the "convergence" of two people. When people come together it is the joining of who they are as persons. The combination of who the spouses are determines to a large extent how they relate. We venture to say it again; how we relate determines our relationships. Who knows whether the unique "pieces of a puzzle", shaping a person, will fit the distinctive "pieces of a puzzle" shaping another person?

Questions, such as "how can I know whether he or she is the right person for me", actually reflect how the "pieces of the puzzle" fit together. Sometimes some aspects of one's personality fit together suitably, but not other characteristics. Trying circumstances have a way of rotating the "pieces of a puzzle", bringing out a different side of a person - a side not known before. At times the person whose "other side" has been brought out may even be surprised by that side of himself or herself. At times the "pieces of the puzzle" of a person's personality fit together in terms of certain worldviews, but then again, certain characteristics of the "pieces of the puzzle" might not match. When a "wrong" or unknown side of someone is brought out that person may look back and say:

- "I do not know what happened to me."
- "I do not even know myself anymore."
- "Where did that come from?"
- "I do not know why I did or said that."
- "I do not know what came over me."

When a suitably fitting "piece of the puzzle" is turned around, the other and lesser known sides of one's personality show up. The other side of that "piece of the puzzle" does not fit his or her spouse's "pieces of the puzzle", and they encounter conflict. When this happens they explode because of issues that ordinarily should not have caused them to get angry, and then they do and say things they regret later. If we need to understand who we are, how we react, what feelings we have and why we have them, it is imperative to comprehend the past that shaped us in this way. If we understood ourselves better, we would be able to better predict how we will react in specific circumstances. Predictable behavior is typically preventable behavior. If we could prevent negative interaction we would be able to protect our emotional intimacy.

It is important to realize that everybody has one or more sides of his or her "puzzle pieces" of personality that are out of "shape." No person is perfect; since birth we have been exposed to people who have hurt and disappointed us. Perhaps one of our parents hurt us; if not a parent, then possibly a teacher. There are also other family members, for example, siblings who could have hurt us. The point is that at some stage in our lives we might have been hurt, some of us more than others. It is a well-known fact that emotionally-wounded people hurt others again. The people who hurt us might not have done it deliberately; they were just bruised themselves. Similarly, we may not wish to hurt our spouses deliberately, but as the saying goes, "hurting people hurt people." If we are emotionally hurting we might well hurt others.

When growing up all of us were exposed to negative experiences in our lives. These events typically repeat themselves and touch on the same topic, again and again; soon a pattern begins to emerge that causes hurt relating to the same topic of our experiences. These topics leave us hurting on a specific issue, and it may be more than one topic, causing us to feel a certain way regarding that issue. The way in which our emotional pain causes us to feel can usually be described by a single concept, such as feelings of: rejection, being abandoned, unloved, abused, picked on, blamed, judged, hated, to be in the way of others, at fault, and so on.

As these repeated painful emotional events happen we have to learn how to minimize the hurt; in this way a coping strategy is developed, and, surprisingly, this strategy is very simple and limited in options. In fact, people tend to react in only one of two ways:

First, some people tend to *adopt* the negative behavior, which they experienced, and they repeat it frequently, for example, most child abusers were abused as children. Many who struggle with alcoholism had an alcoholic parent or an alcoholic family member who played an important role in their early years. Logically, one would think that someone who had such a horrible childhood experience would never wish to put someone else through the same experience – but it still happens. In such cases it is incredible that people would become like that which they hated; they now inflict the same emotional injury upon others that they received. Healing is needed to prevent these destructive behaviors from continuing. These negative behaviors destroy others for certain, but many times they can also destroy their own lives.

Second and alternatively, people may hate the negative experience they endured so much that they become *oversensitive* to even a hint of that undesirable emotional experience. Often they vow never to tolerate that behavior again. Related behavior, which by all counts would be quite normal and acceptable, is immediately interpreted as the same type of behavior against which the vow had been taken. At the slightest indication of that harmful behavior they overreact as they have become oversensitive to it.

Let us use a fictitious example: A woman's dad was an alcoholic and was never home when she needed him. Every time there was conflict in the house, which was often, he walked out to go somewhere to abuse alcohol; he was never there for her, and he was not even aware of her personal struggles. He barely knew of the financial difficulties he caused her and her mother. It was of no use try to talk to him about it, because the moment the conversation about these issues started he simply left for a drink and he often disappeared for days on end. His daughter felt "abandoned." When she had trouble at school her father could not even be located to deal with it. As an adult she will in all probability either adopt the behavior of her father and also become an alcoholic or become addicted to some other substance.

Sometimes people adopt the negative behavior more subtly. They may not abuse alcohol, but they too may become unwilling to face issues and walk out or withdraw whenever issues are in need of being addressed. Alternatively, she will become oversensitive to any situation with the slightest indication of "being abandoned." She would be oversensitive towards abandonment to such an extent that she would interpret just about any related behavior as abandonment. When she hurts, she will hurt severely.

She is now an adult in a relationship with Mr. Right, also a fictitious person. One night he worked late. That afternoon the dishwasher broke and she desperately needed him. There was water all over the place. She could not find the right tools to fix anything and she did not know what to do. Mr. Right was at work and unaware of the drama at home. When he arrived home late, a very angry wife greeted him. He did not work late often, and he did tell her that he would be late that day. In the past he always supported her and was usually there when she needed him. He did not have a drinking problem, and he did not go out with the "boys", leaving her alone. Had he been married to someone else, this situation would not have been a problem – someone else would not necessarily have the same sensitivity of abandonment and in such dire need to be assisted.

In this case it is a problem, and she exploded. She might not even know why she exploded. She might think that she was angry because he was late, but in fact, she erupted because she was hyper-sensitive to people not being available when she needed them. He apologized and thought the issue was resolved, but she kept on harassing him about it. He asked her for a bit of space and calm, as he did not know why she was so upset. Asking for space, however, was the worst thing he could do, as she was oversensitive to anyone wanting to leave in the face of conflict – that's what her dad used to do, and she hated that.

Mr. Right had no idea why she was so mad at him. Yes, the dishwasher broke down and there was a serious problem, but that was not his fault. She blamed him "for not being there for her." He thought her accusations were unfair, as he was generally there for her and did not often work late. Her emotional pain seemed to be disproportionate to the issue at hand. Their emotional intimacy was taking a severe knock. Then suddenly she brought up examples of him not being there for her in the past. These examples, however, did not seem to illustrate to him that he was not there for her. During the next week he quoted these examples to some of his male and female friends, all agreeing that they were not illustrative of what she claimed. No one else could see her point, as they were not oversensitive to the issue. She felt frustrated and alone yet again. He could not understand why their emotional intimacy was failing and "misfiring."

She actually exploded as she was "reliving" and re-experiencing the pain her dad inflicted on her. Mr. Right's not being there during her need was similar to what her father did. His not being there for her was not the issue per se; the real issue was that his not being there triggered her memory of her early years; her early years are the issue. All those angry emotions were relived. She thinks that her husband is the problem (because he was not there for her), but she does not realize that his behavior was just the trigger not the bomb.

Emotional pain is often accumulative and piling up. It seems as if you have bumped yourself and it resulted in a bruise. If someone bump against the same spot again, just slightly and accidently, the pain far exceeds the pain from the slight bump, as there was already a serious bruise. The previous injury and the current one together contribute to the pain accumulatively. Had that little "bump" taken place on a different part of the body, it would not have been painful at all. The person who caused the light bump had no idea why the bumped person reacted so severely; after all, it was just a little "bump."

Even though these bruises can be very old in relationships, they would still be painful, as the bruises were still there, and not healed. We might even have forgotten where they came from, or who inflicted them. Sometimes we even forget that we had them. When someone thumps the old bruise, the reaction is "worthy" of the pain as the pain is from the old bruise *plus* that of the new bump. Now there will be conflict, feelings get hurt and things go wrong; Emotional intimacy fails and "misfires."

If a spouse knew about the old bruise, he or she could be careful in that area; knowing of that old bruise can assist a spouse to understand that he or she was not responsible for all the pain. The guilty parties were actually those who caused the original wound – not the person who lightly bumped him or her later on. Both "adoption of" and "over-sensitivity to" negative behavior is unhealthy and harmful for our relationships and us. They cause us to experience hurt and wound emotions repeatedly. They can confuse our spouses, who might have no idea what was going on. Our "adopted" behavior and touchiness hurts our spouses. We have to understand that in the cases of the "adoption" of negative behavior and hypersensitivity over against certain behavior the events that resulted in our blowing up *were simply the triggers – not the causes*. This is serious; in most relationships we fight about the triggers, believing them to be the sources of the conflict.

She thought that Mr. Right was the cause of her pain as he was not there for her when she needed him. He was indeed the trigger that sparked her feeling that way. She might not be aware of the fact, however, that he was only the trigger and not the cause. Her father was the cause. She was reliving the accumulative pain of her father not being there for her, and the trigger, therefore, irritated either the adopted negative behavior, or the touchiness towards certain behavior.

To be able to conquer these issues and heal past wounds, we have to figure out what the root causes are. She could train and remind Mr. Right all the time, but it would not solve her issue of oversensitivity. The problem was simply that he was the trigger and not the root cause. Dealing with him is not going to solve the problem because in this case he is not the problem.

Let us assume that someone walks around with a little pebble in his or her shoe; the pebble hurts this person's foot terribly. After a while the pebble causes him or her to limp and lean over to one side as he or she walked trying to mitigate the pain. Before long the person's back will be aching. To lean to one side when walking alleviates the foot pain very effectively; before long the foot won't hurt anymore. The person forgets that there was any problem with the foot as it no longer hurts. Now, however, the person suffers from backache. The logical conclusion seems to be that the problem is the aching back, as it is, after all, where the pain is.

Consequently, the person goes to a chiropractor who examined the aching back and, sure enough, the back is leaning irregularly towards one side. The doctor fixes the "problem" quickly, but not surprisingly, after a few weeks the person is back at the doctor's office so he or she treats the back "problem" once again. After months of doctor's visits the doctor requests x-rays, and they revealed that the spine was indeed leaning unnaturally towards one side. An inferior chiropractor would keep on fixing the "problem" again and again, but a superior one would ask, "Why is this problem recurring, and what is the real root cause?"

The backache is simply the trigger – not the real problem. The pebble in the shoe is the real problem. No treatment will prevent the back pain for any length of time until the pebble is found and removed.

When we deal with problems in our relationships, we often deal only with the triggers and not with the real problems. We often do not even know about "the pebble"; since the back hurts, it draws the attention. We think that the back is the problem, but it is not. To treat the back pain permanently we need to remove the pebble in the shoe.

Mr. Right's confusion about his wife's anger was justified. *He was her "back pain" and not "the pebble."* He did not even know there was "a pebble." When he was blamed for her feelings she regarded him as the problem. Emotional intimacy will fail and "misfire" if we confuse the triggers as the root causes, and then real problems would not be solved. This is why we often fight over the same topics; over and over again.

By understanding our past, we can identify the real and true sources of conflict and deal with the "pebbles." Understanding will assist us to figure out why we feel and react the way we do. If we can ascertain which areas and behaviors are sensitive, we will be able to identify for certain the issues to be faced.

Typically, mature and understanding adults learn how to deal with each other's problems. If he has sensitive areas or negative behaviors in areas where she does not, she can learn to be cautious around that area, and he can learn to change that behavior. She can simply learn not to go there. It does not make sense to go prodding and pushing at a spouse's bruises.

The challenging situations are those where one person's sensitivity or adopted negative behavior coincides with the other person's sensitivity or adopted negative behavior. These are the issues where we can guarantee to expect serious trouble. As stated before, most predictable behavior is preventable. We can begin by figuring out where we are hypersensitive and apt to fall into negative behaviors. Once we know this, we could see whether his issues coincide with hers. Both parties now need to be educated about these wounds. They need to be led down the path of healing and restoration. At the very least, we would understand what was really going on when there are explosions in certain areas.

When these problems are very painful, we often wish to give up on the relationship. We have to remember that pain, which is experienced, is often accumulated pain, not just the pain caused by this relationship. These wounds have been carried over from previous encounters. Your spouse is not necessarily to blame – he or she has only provided the trigger. The answer is certainly not to be found in a new relationship with a different person. Of course, a relationship with someone else, who does not have the same issue, will not have the same problem, but all people have issues. In fact, one would just be trading one problem for another. The solution is actually the healing of the wounds, the learning and knowledge of the skills to deal with the sensitive issues in an uplifting manner; let us get rid of the "pebble."

Please understand, as the illustration pointed out, that we are not talking about enduring unacceptable behavior. Mr. Right did not do anything wrong. He informed his wife that he would be a bit late. It is assumed that we are dealing with normal and relationally healthy people. Obviously, if your spouse is beating you, on drugs, or an alcoholic he or she has the problem. This chapter does not deal with these kinds of issues. If you face such situations, please get professional help.

In the picture below we have two grids, one for each person. Check marks represent issues, either adopted negative behaviors or sensitivities that do not coincide with the other person's issues. Notice that one person's check mark is in an area where the other person does not have a check mark. This person's check marks are issues, but they are not related to the spouse's issues. We usually deal with them by avoiding that area. These are problems, but people generally tend to be able to work towards a solution. Where two issues coincide we have an "X." We know this relationship will have real trouble in this area. If the issue of one person is different from that of the other person, one person's issue acts as a trigger for the other person's issue. If his issue is the same as hers, the destruction is even worse, because a negative spiral can occur where one issue feeds the other person's issue and vice versa. The issues simply keep on feeding each other. Well-fed issues grow.

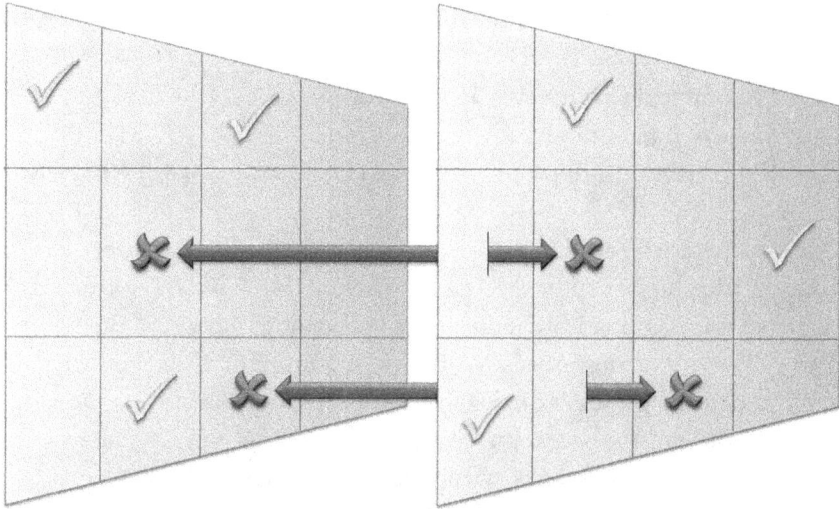

In the relationship depicted above, both spouses have issues, but the issues that will cause problems are the ones that coincide; the arrows indicate coincidences. Where coincidences occur, one person's issue tends either to fuel or trigger the other person's issue. If a behavior causes a person to hurt, he or she will then either repeat the behavior, or will be sensitive to it and will explode. The explosion will cause the other person either to repeat the behavior, or to be oversensitive to it and to "explode" too. Now we have two "explosions." The fighting over these issues will be recurring, and will follow a predictable pattern.

We note that when people repeatedly fight, these struggles typically involve the same issues. The way they fight may also be the same every time. It is as if the conflict happens in a pre-programmed way. Therapists often want couples to fight when they are in session so that the therapist can observe how they fight. It is easier for an uninvolved third party to observe the pattern of fighting. Once the pattern of combating is identified, disruption of that pattern changes the whole dynamic of the struggle. If we knew how we fought, we could prevent it from happening that way. If couples fight according to the same pattern it is like déjà vu. We are able to recognize often-repeated issues by the following examples:

- "Here we go again ..."
- "This always happens ..."
- "This is pointless ..."
- "We have been over this before ..."
- "You always do this or say that ..."
- "I cannot deal with this anymore ..."
- "I have had enough of this ..."
- "You never do this or say that ..."

If the pattern of fights develops in the same way every time, it will be predictable, but it will also be preventable. We have to find out what these issues are, and whether they coincide with any of the spouse's issues. Touchy areas need to be desensitized. Adopted negative behaviors need to be unlearned. Understanding our past holds the key.

There is no point in blaming a spouse nor is such blame warranted if we are the ones with the issue. These issues were present long before the relationship even started. It just so happened that his issues directly corresponded with hers. Exploring who each person is and discovering what each one's issues are is invaluable to identify the root causes of emotional intimacy "misfires" and confusion. How can we heal a wound if we do not know it is a wound, or if we do not know where the wound is? This is primarily a process of self-discovery and exploration.

Once we understand our own issues we can explore and discover our partners' issues as well. This, however, is not the end of the road as there is one more vital step; it is important to learn how his issues have an impact on her issues and vice versa. The "misfire" and failure of emotional intimacy is all about the combination of issues between people; this combination holds the key to understand how a relationship would be influenced by the issues. Time is better spent to focus on the root causes of failure and the misfiring of intimacy than to waste time on the triggers.

Once the root causes are healed the triggers won't have anything to set off or to trigger. The impact on emotional intimacy is less negative on us by talking about our past issues and how they affect the current relationship than is fighting with each other. In this way a couple can form a team to fight a common enemy together; the distant past. Emotional intimacy benefits tremendously if we do not regard each other as "the enemy." Our spouses were not present in our "past", that is our distant past. When we met our spouses we already possessed our issues. Our spouses already owned their issues. Blaming each other is pointless and only serves to ruin emotional intimacy. Dealing with the root causes of the failure and "misfires", and realizing that the root causes are not always what triggered the pain makes a great deal more sense.

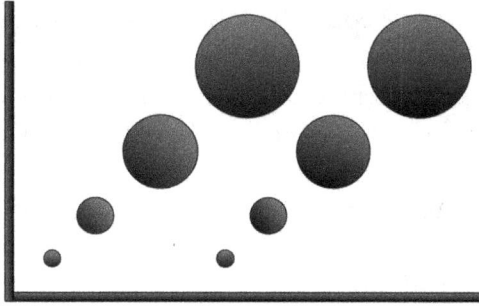

❦ CHAPTER TEN ❧

THE CORRELATION BETWEEN THE LEVEL OF TALKING AND EMOTIONAL INTIMACY

Discussion and talking is very important for emotional intimacy. The art of talking has many elements which makes an impact on emotional intimacy, for example, the tone of voice is often more important than what we actually say. Certain topics of conversation influence emotional intimacy more than others. If we wish to build up emotional intimacy it simply makes sense to speak about topics that have a positive impact on emotional intimacy rather than attempting to enhance emotional intimacy by talking about topics which do not successfully foster emotional intimacy. How we talk, and what we discuss often indicate the level of emotional intimacy between the speakers. Talking and discussions are a great deal more difficult than what they seem. There are all kinds of communication pitfalls that could cause misunderstanding and unclear communication.

How about spending some time thinking of the following concepts and asking yourselves what initially comes to mind when you think about them: "Sun", "sky" and "car." When you thought about these words, did you see something, or did you think about the letters that made up the words, s-u-n, s-k-y, and c-a-r? Did you contemplate how these words were written or did you think about the sounds that make up the words? Most people do not think about letters and sounds, but they see something. People think by way of thoughts, ideas, feelings, and concepts; we see the hot, bright sun, or perhaps a sunset. We see a scene of the sky, perhaps blue or maybe filled with white puffy clouds. We see a particular car complete with its shape, color and men may sometimes even see the brand of the car; this is not to say that there are no lady car lovers. As you probably noticed, our brains most often work visually.

The letters and words most often do not even enter into our minds. Words are tools we use to communicate, and words are not actual concepts, ideas and thoughts. Words simply represent them.

This is what makes communication so difficult. There is no way that a person can convey what he or she thinks to another so that they both think exactly the same thought in the say way. One person cannot express his or her feelings to someone else so that the other person feels the same thing. So, how do we communicate our thoughts and feelings to other people? The only way to communicate our thoughts and feelings to others is to translate or encode them into words, drawings, facial expressions, body language, etc. We literally encode what we wish to communicate. Letters, words, and sounds are simply codes for thoughts, concepts, ideas, objects, actions and feelings.

This is *the first barrier* to communication; sometimes we do not encode correctly what we think. Either we do not know the correct word, pick a mistaken word, or the word we picked matches the thought only partially. Sometimes we even use conflicting codes, for example, the first code, or words we may say is, "I am not angry", but the second code, the voice tone may express, "I am angry!" If the words are shouted and a fist is shaken in the air it is a third code. Thus, the coding process may introduce errors into our communication. Since listeners cannot read speakers' minds they only have access to the codes used to communicate. If the speaker uses wrong or conflicting codes the listener hears or sees a different concept or feeling than what the speaker attempted to communicate. We have already seen that men and women hear different messages from what the other gender sent, due to gender differences. Now we see that wrong coding of the speaker can also result in a different message from the one intended.

The *second barrier* to communication is *the decoding process*. The person receiving the codes also thinks in thoughts, concepts, ideas and feelings rather than words, letters and sounds. For the receiver to understand the intended message he or she needs to process the codes received; they have to be decoded. The process used by the sender to encode thoughts and concepts now has to be reversed by the receiver. Codes need to be decoded back into thoughts, concepts, ideas and feelings. This is very difficult to do, since the sent codes could have contained errors and contradictions. To complicate matters even further, the decoder might also make mistakes in the decoding process. The decoding process is influenced by cultural differences; the way people were brought up, fears, prior experiences, mindsets, moods, contexts, and all kinds of other influences.

For decades a simple, but successful solution has been used in the computer industry; modems and fax machines send signals to other modems or fax machines. While the signal travels through the wires noise is introduced due to interference, for example. This noise corrupts the messages. To solve the problem engineers programmed the machines to use "error correction." When modems or fax machines receive a signal, they pause every few seconds to send back a chunk of information they have just received, so that the sending device can verify the information. If the contents are verified, the transmission continues, but if not, the same information is resent. Human communication is more complex than that of machines. Perhaps we need this simple solution even more than modems; we can do the same! After every few sentences or paragraphs we can simply ask the sender or speaker whether what we heard was, in fact, what was sent. If what we heard was what was said, the speaker feels that they are being listened to and understood. Incorrect communication is prevented and mis-understanding cleared up. If what was heard was not what was intended, it provides the speaker the opportunity to correct the communication error. The following questions may be asked to accomplish this task:

- "Did I hear correctly when I heard...?"
- "You seem to have said ...; is this correct?"
- "This is what I heard...; is that what you meant?"
- "I perceive you as ...; is my perception correct?"
- "Your tone of voice indicated ...; is that what you feel?"

This technique is not important just for accurate communication; it is also important for emotional intimacy. When people reflect on what they hear and ask if they followed it correctly, it helps the communicator to feel understood. Experiencing comprehension or feeling understood helps to bond the speaker and the listener. Emotional intimacy can be improved by something as simple as this.

Reflecting what was heard back to the speaker shows that people are not just listening, but that they are really "tuned in" and interested in what is said. It is a more intimate way of listening that fosters the relationship. Women especially appreciate this very much. The more effort invested in listening the deeper the emotional intimacy grows. This is one of the differences between listening and hearing. This is the difference between, "I told him or her that ...", and, "we connected when we spoke about ..." Listening well is as important in talking. There is a direct correlation between understanding each other, hearing correctly, feeling listened to, on the one hand, and the depth of emotional intimacy, on the other. The level of listening communicates the level of interest and caring that the listener feels towards the speaker.

Even if both the speaker and the listener communicate well, the topic or level of communication also correlates directly with emotional intimacy. There are a number of different levels of communication that takes place. Some levels of communication are not intimate at all while others are intimate and enhance emotional intimacy:

First, there is *the cliché*. A cliché is a trite or commonplace phrase that does not require an answer or requires only a set answer. Examples of clichés would be, "How are you?" answered with, "Fine thanks." At this level of communication people do not really listen to one another. They are merely going through the motions of being polite. When people ask others how they are they are not really interested how the other person is; it is just a form of greeting, for example, saying, "Hello." To prove the point, try this test: The next time you go to work and someone asks you, "How are you?" smile brightly, use a very happy and upbeat tone of voice and say, "Bad, thank you!" Most people will not even notice what you have said. Many might even reply with another cliché, for example, "Me too", "Good", "Glad to hear that", etc.

This level of communication has no place with those with whom emotional intimacy is sought. It is often described as fake and not genuine. This does not mean that this level of communication is of no use; it has its place – you hardly have the time every day to listen intently to every person you rub shoulders with. Sometimes you are dealing with people with whom you have very shallow relationships, which naturally provide a low level of emotional intimacy.

While visiting a car dealership to purchase a new car it is not in anybody's interest to open up and have a heart to heart talk. After all, the buyer does not wish to open up and tell the salesperson how much he or she is really willing to pay for the car. Neither does the salesperson want to open up and tell the buyer what the absolute minimum he or she is willing to accept for the car. There are many situations and relationships where emotional intimacy is limited for good reasons. As it has been said before, too much emotional intimacy with people who are not close to us is inappropriate.

In marriages communication needs to go deeper than the cliché level. In fact, if your spouse "catches you out" asking a question, without you really wishing to know the answer, emotional intimacy will decrease. This is because the level of communication between people is proportional to the level of emotional intimacy between them. If people wish to know how much emotional intimacy exists between them they can merely examine the level of communication between them. If we wish to obtain more emotional intimacy we have to increase the level of talking; we have to move onto the deepest levels of talking.

At what level do you and your spouse communicate? Do you really want to know how your spouse is doing when you ask the question? Do you ask the question in passing or does your body language indicate that you are waiting for a genuine response and that you are willing to take the time to listen?

Second there is *sharing facts*. Sharing facts is simply a little deeper than clichés. Very little or no emotional intimacy is required to share facts. The level of emotional intimacy required at each communication level is proportional to the growth in emotional intimacy that that level of communication generates. When little or no emotional intimacy is involved in our communication there is little or no benefit to the emotional intimacy between the communicators. The opposite is also true; at the level we share facts, for example, the weather, news, and reports of our daily events, our meetings, our shopping, etc., nothing personal is revealed.

Often couples get stuck at this level of communication, much to the frustration of the wife in particular.

When the husband and wife get home the conversation may start with a cliché, for example, "How was your day?" Subsequently, the conversation should go one level deeper as one of them shares the events of the day. At this level of communication the only topics of conversation revolve around the events of the day; however, communication of both levels can take place between any two people, as the level of emotional intimacy is actually insignificant. Thus, this kind of conversation has an insignificant impact on emotional intimacy. Most couples communicate and talk at this level and, as a result, their emotional intimacy suffers. If there is a desire to increase emotional intimacy there has to be more emotional intimacy involved in communication and talking. The discussions have to be more personal. The growth of emotional intimacy requires that people talk more about thoughts and feelings and less about the news and daily events.

Third there are *ideas and opinions*. At this level of communication people take the facts and news, being shared at the previous level, and complement them with personal ideas and opinions. Instead of merely talking about "external" events they now share "internal" ideas and opinions. They disclose and share themselves.

It actually takes a relational risk to share ideas and opinions; one risks being ridiculed, being giggled at, being disagreed with, or possibly having those ideas used against one in the future. In exchange for the risk, however, there is also reward. The reward is fulfillment, relational intimacy, and bonding. For example, the external event was that Sarah laughed, to use a fictitious illustration. Consequently, at the third level Sarah's companion shares the previous level's news about the laughter, which was an event, but then he moves from level two to level three by adding what he thought of her laughter. Now they share something more personal; their thoughts about the event. No one can question whether Sarah laughed or not, but thoughts about the event can be questioned, challenged, disagreed with, and so forth. This kind of communication requires more risk-taking than simply reporting that Sarah laughed. It also informs the listener more about your thoughts and opinions about the event, which is obviously more personal. Talking about that which is personal enhances emotional intimacy. These thoughts may reflect that Sarah's laughter was inappropriate for the boardroom executive meeting, or that the CEO's joke about that event was hilarious. Either way, more personal sharing of thoughts connect people more intimately.

Shared experiences alone do not create profound bonding. I fly fairly often. Waiting in line for the security screening with a multitude of other passengers does not bond us together. Although we all share the same experience, it does not create an intimate connection between us. We merely experience an event together. Physical togetherness and closeness by themselves do not imply emotional intimacy.

Let us now for a moment imagine that a crazy man starts shooting into the crowd of people waiting to be screened. There would be chaos and passengers would fall to the ground; there would be shouting and perhaps soft crying and people would be hurt; some would be assisting others. Now, how profound would the bond be between this group of passengers, compared to the bonding of the same group prior to the mad man's entrance?

Or to use another example, what would be the difference between the bonds of the passengers whose plane crashed into the Hudson River in New York, and the bonds of another group of passengers whose plane landed uneventfully and safely at LaGuardia airport in New York? What causes the difference? The first group shared personal experiences; they cared for one another, but most of all, they shared similar feelings, thoughts and emotions. They did not even have to say anything as they shared in-depth bonding because of mutual personal and sensitive feelings. The passengers that landed safely only shared an experience that did not include anything personal or any tender or profound feelings. When we communicate we can talk about events and experiences while not really making an impact on emotional intimacy, or we can convey to one another how we feel about, and what we think of those events that boost emotional intimacy.

If we communicate in this personal way the discussion now turns to private and personal thoughts and feelings about the event. A person now discusses something about his or her mind, from the inside, and a risk is being taken; the person now becomes genuine, real and unpretentious, and that creates emotional intimacy.

Now think of an irritating person with an opinion about everything, making it known to everybody at every occasion. To make matters worse, it seems as if very few people agree with these opinions.

This causes a nuisance to any conversation, often stifling a discussion. Generally, people are too scared to voice their own opinions in this person's presence as he or she may contradict loudly and passionately what anyone else would say. These people think that only their opinions matter as only their views are valid and the others are wrong. No one seems to speak intimately with such a person for any length of time; he or she drains one's emotional intimacy. This kind of conversation is usually recognized when everyone else looks at each other without the opinionated person noticing these glances. How then should we share our thoughts, ideas, and opinions to enhance emotional intimacy?

Such an irritating person's communication is certainly not a surefire way to build up emotional intimacy; rather it is a surefire way to misfire, to suffocate intimacy. The level of communication, the level of personal disclosure of inner thoughts and feelings, needs to be appropriate for the level of emotional intimacy already shared. When you become personal and intense with others with whom there is not much emotional intimacy it becomes awkward very quickly and they are put down. It is strange, though, that most people know this, yet have no idea that the opposite is also valid: It is obvious that emotional intimacy would decline if we never talk about anything personal. The very word "intimacy" screams personal.

When we want to build up emotional intimacy our communication has to become more personal, but at a point appropriate for the level of shared emotional intimacy. The idea is to develop emotional intimacy with someone close, to embark on a journey of exploration with a spouse that takes you both to new heights, to new levels of profound emotional intimacy. Become more personal and intimate by sharing more about what you think and feel to invite your spouse to become more personal and intimate, and share what he or she thinks and feels. Becoming more personal has to be accepted by both, and it has to be reciprocated to increase emotional intimacy. Anyone who over-shadows conversation, as in the previous example, will "misfire" in terms of emotional intimacy. Sharing our internal feelings and thoughts should be the opening of the door to let our spouses know that we were willing to take the risk and to make ourselves vulnerable, and that would be safe for them to take that risk too. By opening the door to our hearts we invite our spouses to come in. It should not be in our interest to indoctrinate our partners, but to gain more insight and understanding of what is taking place inside the personal lives of our spouses.

When we fall in love there is initially rapid growth in emotional intimacy; why? The growth occurs because the couple explores one another and gets to know each other. They do not explore events and experiences by themselves; rather, each one explores the other. It stands to reason that after a few years of marriage there is not much left to learn about each other. Yet, anyone will testify that he or she does not fully understand his or her spouse. There is actually a lot more to explore after all. Exploration simply gets more difficult as time goes by, because the only way to discover something new about one's spouse is to go deeper and to get more personal; the surface has already been explored to death. It just does not make sense to keep on exploring the same surface while the gold is buried beneath. Why do we continue to talk about and explore news and events when there are intimate opinions, thoughts and feelings waiting to be discovered behind every event?

So why not ask what our spouses think and feel about what was just said? How about attempting to understand them better? Whether or not we agree with their opinions and views is not relevant here; the aim is to learn who they are, what and how they think and feel. It is the feeling of being listened to and feeling understood that is a surefire way to great emotional intimacy in romantic relationships. We do not have to be afraid to tell our spouses what we think and feel as long as a safe and accepting environment exists in the relationship. We can also let our spouses know that it is safe for them to open up, to go down to a more intimate level where our thoughts and feelings are stowed away. We can request them to reciprocate in this safe environment because all we seek is a glimpse of their inside, their intimate feelings and thoughts. Talking about how we feel and what we think is not done to be judged, but to understand, to share, and to support. Connections from "inside to inside" is the fabric of emotional intimacy.

We can discard our fear as we experience the benefit of more personal emotional intimacy, and we can increase the risk by going a bit deeper and getting more personal in our intimate communication. We can share more than just news and events; emotional intimacy exists when we share personal emotions and thoughts. We can also encourage our spouses to do the same.

We have to remember that intimate sharing involves risk. When our spouses take that risk it is very important to reward the risk by also sharing our intimate lives and to open up. If judging, mocking, arguing, or invalidating violates the risk of our spouses, the risk-taking towards intimacy will cease. It cannot be said enough; emotional intimacy by its very nature is personal. Emotional intimacy cannot exist without getting personal. Just talking about events and news is simply not getting personal.

The communication between two romantics has to deepen to include sharing their inner selves if emotional intimacy is to flourish. This is done by opening up the deepest chambers of our hearts to each other. Secrets do not exist at this level of talking, because secrets mean that something is held back, access is barred and the vault is locked up with our intimate feelings and personal thoughts inside. There can be complete openness with one another without blaming or judging. This level of intimate talking is filled with mutual respect, loyalty, understanding, and support. This level of communicating takes place between two people who are trustworthy and who feel safe.

There is a direct correlation between the level of talking and listening taking place and the level of emotional intimacy experienced. Superficial emotional intimacy is a consequence of superficial talking and listening. Talking about the inner self or soul leads to the formation of soul mates. If we talk at the level of desired emotional intimacy this personal emotional intimacy will become a reality. Misfire or surefire emotional intimacy is your choice; talk according to the level of emotional intimacy you desire and need.

❧ CHAPTER ELEVEN ❦

THE ART OF TALKING FOR SUREFIRE EMOTIONAL INTIMACY

Talking is an art and some are masters of it; they can sell ice to Eskimos and sand to desert dwellers. Some speak so eloquently that it is a pure joy to listen to them. Then again there are people who speak beautifully, but say little. There is no substance to what is said. People tend to hang on their lips for only a short while before realizing that there is nothing worthwhile to listen to.

There is also an art in talking to develop emotional intimacy. This art is not measured by poetic speech, or by the frequency of alliteration or sound repetition, nor by the eloquent use of figures of speech. It has been shown that the level or depth of openness, honestly, vulnerability, support, and genuineness measures this art, and the care involved in the conversation. It is how deeply we talk and how personal we get that determines the impact on emotional intimacy.

The art of conversation involves talking as well as listening. Fortunately it is an art that can be learned and practiced. The more determined we are to transform talking into an art and the more it is practiced the better we communicate. The art of conversing for surefire emotional intimacy engages the techniques of personal and deep communication.

For example, both spouses get home from work and greet each other with a cliché like, "How was your day?" Typically the conversation then deepens slightly to share the news of the day. As we have seen before, most people simply continue the conversation at this level rather than going deeper to insights, feelings and opinions; they do not risk opening up, or sharing anything personal, but they also forgo the reward of surefire emotional intimacy. In a way they may be content, but they are not fulfilled and they are certainly not as happy as they could be.

Another example can be used to make an important point: When a knife slips and cuts open one's finger, the healing process produces a scar and scar tissue is thicker than normal skin as it is there to protect the finger. The side effect of scar tissue, however, is that some sensitivity to touch is lost; one does not feel as much there as before. Our hearts or emotional lives operate similarly.

When things hurt us repeatedly our hearts build "walls", "scar tissue" for protection. This is beneficial as it protects us from more hurt in the future. The reason why these "walls" are so effective at protecting us is because they keep people out. If no one is let in we cannot get hurt. Unfortunately, these walls have the pricey side effect of preventing more emotional intimacy. *Sadly we cannot enjoy both iron clad protection and surefire intimacy at the same time.* We have to make a choice between protection with less emotion (and intimacy), and more feelings (and intimacy) with less protection. If a person takes the risks that intimate relationships demand there may be hurt as that is the risk one takes. On the other hand, that risk may be rewarded with exciting relational bliss. If a risk is not taken, a person gets protection from possible hurt, but at the same time one also forgoes the reward. To complicate things even more, those walls of protection built because of hurt caused by a negative relationship also negatively affect relationships with others. Walls from embittered childhoods steal away future sensitivity for wonderful fulfilling feelings in current relationships. Those alienating walls have to be broken down to restore the sensitivity needed to enjoy the rewards great passionate and romantic relationships offer. Braking down these walls, however, entails the risk of being hurt again – that is the risk we take.

Numerous times her father has cheated on her mother. As a little girl she has also experienced some of the pain her mother has suffered. She remembers the uncertainly; she can almost still hear the fighting that took place. Every time when the dust settled after an affair her mother forgave her father and restored the relationship. The next time he was caught with another woman, it broke her mother's heart even further, and this cycle continued for many years. Her mother built up a lot of emotional scar tissue. By the fifth or sixth occasion she had so many walls built around her heart, deadening her feelings that she was not hurt that much again; actually, she even expected it; the walls did their job well, she was protected from pain.

Unknown to the little girl, who lived through all the heartaches, she also built walls as her heart was scarred in the same way. Now, years later she got married. Her husband was a wonderful person and never cheated on her. Their relationship, however, floundered against the protective walls that had ground around her feelings in her heart. It seemed as though she could not allow herself to truly open up to him; she kept him at a distance, probably because of her latent fear of being hurt. She did not trust him, even though she did not have anything against him to justify her mistrust. Others labeled her as "Mrs. Detective" as she verified and checked everything her husband did and said. After listening to her story and seeing the husband's frustration I thought that we were dealing with some scar tissue left behind from her parents. She could not bring herself to love her dad completely and to come close to him as he cheated and had been kicked out of their home repeatedly during the latter part of that marriage. She did not know whether she had a dad to love; every time she got close to him and loved him his cheating "took" him from her by being kicked out again. She was hurt and walls were built, resulting in more scar tissue.

Without her being able to verbalize what was going on her fears were being projected onto her husband; what if he was not for real? What if he cheated? What if he left her? She knew that she did not want, or did not have the strength to go through such pain again. So she did what was emotionally logical; to prevent the potential pain she did not allow herself to get too close to him. It worked up to a point as she was protected, but the price of her protection was too high; she missed out on the blissful feelings and sensitivity from loving and being loved.

Her yearning for emotional fulfillment and love, however, was not quenched. Such yearnings cannot be quenched by anything other than loving and being loved. Every human being has the desire to love and to be loved. Without loving and being loved we will never feel fulfilled; there will always be a void. Her yearning could not be stifled, as the two needs of protection and love are in opposition and a choice between the two has to be made. That choice was between the following two possibilities: Protection with shallower love and intimacy, and love and affection with little protection. For someone who has been hurt so deeply and so frequently, this was a terribly difficult decision to make.

Choosing protection will result in a never ending gnawing that unfulfilled love generates. Choosing deeper love and emotional intimacy will result in the gnawing of the fear of being hurt. If the latter option was chosen and she does not get hurt by her husband that fear will eventually go away. So choosing deeper love and emotional intimacy over protection is always the better decision in the long run (as long as you spouse is relationally safe). The advantage of this decision is very evident since the choice is between a gnaw (of unfulfilled love) that never dissipates and a gnaw (of fear of being hurt) that may very well fade away. Hurting people can often not see the advantage of the latter decision because they may not have tasted deeper love and emotional intimacy, yet they know the fear and hurt very well.

Everything was about to change the day she started to practice the art of talking. Practicing the art of talking introduced a minor change in her experience of a bit more emotional intimacy and that change led to further and more profound changes. Consequently, after some time she found healing and their relationship flourished and their emotions were transformed into depths of intimacy.

As long as both parties take equal risks, and both feel safe in the relationship, it is less dicey to take more risks; the experience of great emotional intimacy is worth the risk. We need to open up and go deep to build emotional intimacy. We need not stop at the "news level" of communication. If it seems too risky to open up and expose ourselves, we can always start with minor risks. If those marginal risks are rewarded we can take more advanced risks. This is how trust develops and emotional intimacy is built.

To illustrate this we can use the following example: Suppose someone you hardly know asks you to borrow $10,000 and you have the money to loan it, would you do it? You probably would not. If the same person, however, asks to borrow just $1, would you do it? You probably would because the risk is small; after all what is a Dollar? Now, if that person pays back the loan the following week a little trust has developed. If he or she requests to borrow another Dollar a few days later it is easier to oblige because there is a little bit of trust which was developed with prior experiences. Suppose over time he or she has taken numerous loans from you and faithfully paid you back as promised every time. Six months down the line the person wishes to borrow $50. Would you lend him or her $50? You probably would, because by now a lot of trust has developed. As long as the person keeps on paying the money back trust keeps on built up. The level of trust gets bigger and bigger every time the person is shown to be trustworthy. If this borrowing and paying back were to continue this relationship would eventually reach the stage where you would be willing to provide a loan of $10,000. If at any stage during the lending and borrowing, however, a repayment was neglected, trust would be broken and the loans would be terminated, and consequently, the relationship would suffer damage.

In general, emotional intimacy and relationships operate in the same way. Instead of money, the currency of the transactions is support, love, sharing, and so forth. Little or no risk means that the relationship would exhibit little or no trust. Trust and emotional intimacy is something that can be built up over time by simply taking small risks and then to increase them when those risks are rewarded with reciprocity, love and intimacy.

People have to take the risk and offer a spouse access to deeper places in the soul. It is easier for a spouse to reciprocate what you have allowed than to be the one to start taking the risk. Offer your ideas, opinions, and feelings on what happened that day. If your spouse sees you taking the risk he or she may also take the risk to open up to you.

When a spouse says something about his or her day, it seems natural to say something about your day. Just sharing things about each other's days, however, prevents the conversation from becoming more personal and thereby hinders the development of emotional intimacy. It is wise to fight the urge to share the news from your day and instead learn the art of taking the news of your spouse's day as conversation starters to become intimate and personal. We could ask questions about the shared news designed to assist our spouses to share how they think and feel about what happened. Here are some sample questions:

- "How did you feel when …?"

- "What should 'John' or 'Suzie' have said or done when …?"
- "Who was correct and why do you think he or she was right in this or that situation?"
- "How does this affect you?"
- "How do you plan to deal with …?"
- "What is your opinion about …?"
- "What did you think about …?"

These are open-ended questions that cannot be answered by a "yes" or a "no." It becomes a conversation to answer these questions, for example. More importantly, these kinds of questions cannot be answered by just talking superficially about what happened. They solicit a spouse to share his or her personal thoughts about the events. They demonstrate that *you are more interested in him or her than in the news of the day*. They compel the discussion to get personal and intimate; a positive necessity for emotional intimacy.

Men particularly do well to realize that these kinds of questions are not intended to provide more information so that a solution can be proposed. These questions are intended to help a person to fathom what is going on inside one's spouse's mind and emotions. Spouses seek to feel listened to and understood; merely talking about events does not provide that. The spouse asking the questions is to feel that his or her partner knows him or her better as a result. These questions are designed to bring their feelings and opinions into the open. It is beneficial for emotional intimacy when feelings and opinions are discussed freely. The art of talking takes a conversation deeper and brings to light insights, emotions and opinions hidden from our view, locked inside the heart. Once a particular event is discussed one simply repeats the process the following day or for the next event.

We would do well to remember that people own one mouth and two ears; perhaps we could listen twice as much as speaking. If a listener does not listen, it is just natural for a speaker to stop speaking. The way in which we listen often determines the depth, duration, and intensity of the discussion. Our spouses are often blamed for not talking to us, when the problem may lie with the way in which we listen and the kind of questions we ask. Master the art of talking to enhance emotional intimacy and your relationship will become a more intimate relationship.

Women can assist men when talking by bringing up just one subject for discussion at a time. Men may feel overwhelmed when too many topics or instructions are given at the same time. When men feel overwhelmed due to listening to multiple subjects, tasks, or instructions at the same time they tend to shut down and stop listening.

Instead of asking a husband how his day was, which sounds to him as too much information to share at one time, it would suit him better to ask something specific about the day; for example, "How did your meeting with John go?" If she doesn't know that he had a meeting that day, other specific questions may be asked, for example, "What was the issue that took a lot of your time today?" In this way, he only has to think about a specific event. Once an answer is provided there are numerous questions one can follow up with to take the conversation into the territory of emotional intimacy.

Talking is an art; encouragement to talk followed by good listening can go a long way to assist in developing this art. This can be done, for example, by using the following phrases:

- "Tell me more about …"
- "That sounds interesting, please elaborate …"
- "I do not understand this, please explain …"

The art of talking specifically to increase emotional intimacy is a twofold approach: First, talking should be steered away from simply sharing news, moving instead towards emotional intimacy, depth and it should be personal. Second, talking this way should be encouraged to happen frequently. This cherished way of talking creates a warm connection between people.

Open-ended questions have been mentioned briefly; they are the keys used to unlock speech. Even emotionally withdrawn people can be moved into conversation by using open-ended questions.

Closed-ended questions do not facilitate conversation as they often have very short answers that will close down the topic. When she asks, "Did your meeting go well?" the only possible answers are; "yes", "no", or "okay", thus closing the topic.

An open-ended question would be, "Tell me about your meeting." This cannot be answered in a closed way by just saying "yes" or "no." Instead, one has to share more than a few words, which could lead to a discussion and many other possible questions to stimulate the discussion even further. Other ways of asking open-ended questions instead of eliciting short "yes", "no", or "okay" answers are: "Which part of the meeting went well?" or, "What about the meeting pleased you most?"

So far we have discussed how to turn ordinary conversations into developing extraordinary dialogues towards emotional intimacy. As the conversion changes from discussing news to discussing emotional intimate feelings and opinions more often this could become the normal, ordinary way in which spouses talk to each other. These conversations can take place anytime, anywhere, and when appropriate continuously. As these talks are personal they are not to be shared with people who do not operate at the appropriate level of emotional intimacy with you. Every time we talk in this way emotional intimacy is generated.

The art of talking for surefire emotional intimacy has one more step: This is more deliberate as it takes more time but yields more emotional intimacy; in fact, it adds a certain spark to emotional intimacy. This type of talking works better when enough time is available and nothing else distracts from the conversation. To facilitate this intimate way of talking place two chairs together to face each other. Sit close enough so that your knees touch and hold hands. Positioning is important because when seated in this way you are in each other's personal space, and being there for any length of time requires emotional intimacy. It fosters trust, openness, and honesty, the building blocks of emotional intimacy.

Your personal space is like a pear shaped bubble around you. People can stand right behind us without being in our personal space as we are used to standing in lines. We line up at the checkout counter in just about every store. It does not bother us. Similarly, the boundaries of our personal space on our left and right sides are close to us. People sit next to us on public transport, airplanes, and chairs. This does not mean that we are getting personal. That pear-shaped bubble, however, does extend further forward. When we face each other and get too close we get uncomfortable rapidly because our personal space has been violated. In romantic relationships we actually like being personal and we permit each other into our personal space because the level of intimacy shared is appropriate for entering into each other's intimate space. Sitting in each other's personal space encourages us to get more personal in our talking.

Once seated inside each other's personal space and your knees touch and you hold hands, the conversation can begin. Maintaining good eye contact is important. Remember gazing in someone's eyes for more than eight seconds without glancing away requires intimacy. Doing so when the level of shared intimacy is appropriate grows emotional intimacy. One of you will ask questions only, while the other merely answers them. There is no need to worry about the opposite as the process is to be reversed later on. The person asking the questions uses the art of talking as outlined in this chapter, asking open-ended questions designed to take the discussion deeper and make it more personal. The only purpose for asking any question is to understand a spouse's heart and emotions better. You may not ask questions to cast blame or to resolve issues. Focus questions on the person answering, and not on the person asking them. It is not an interrogation, however.

For example, it is not appropriate after an argument to ask, "Why do you hate me?" In fact, questions to supply reasons why some-body did something are better not asked here. The person asking the questions wishes to find out how his or her spouse feels. Even if answers cause hurt, still just ask questions to understand your spouse better. This requires tremendous risk because we may hear what we do not want to hear. It is important to ask for the sole purpose of understanding your spouse better. If not, your spouse is not going to open up and answer your questions deeply, thoroughly, and honestly. To answer questions in this manner also requires great risk. Be a safe listener and the speaker will say more and allow you deeper into his or her heart.

These talks are meant for regular use, especially when the relationship goes well. It should not be associated with the dreaded, "We need to talk …" "We need to talk" usually means "I need to tell you something, accuse you, or grill you." The art of talking however is not about you; it is about understanding your spouse. This way of talking works well after a loss of emotional intimacy due to fights, etc., but that should be the exception. Good questions to start a conversation may be:

- "How do you feel about our relationship right now?"

- "What is working about our relationship?"
- "What do you enjoy most about us?"

It is a good idea to ask questions about the answers given, but only to better understand your spouse. Once you get into the habit of talking in this way you may feel more confident and brave enough to ask high-risk questions to diagnose and measure the satisfaction of your relationship. Please be careful asking these kinds of questions, as honest answers may hurt. Answers may even be shocking. In addition, answers may blame, but we still have to stick to the rules of the conversation:

1. Whether you agree with expressed blame or not, the person asking the questions may only ask questions to understand his or her spouse better, period.
2. The person asking the questions may not provide answers or make statements (please do not break this rule by making a statement through a question such as: "Do you think it was fair of you to …?", or stated as an open-ended question: "Tell me what was fair about you doing or saying …?")
3. Question may not be asked for any other reason, but to understand a spouse's heart or emotions. So, when he or she says, "It is all your fault that …," you may not ask, "Why do you feel that way," or "Do you think it is fair to blame me?" It may be better to ask, "So you feel rejected by me?" or "So you feel let down by me?" Once it is certain how he or she feels, it can be followed up with an open-ended question like, "Tell me about other times when you felt this way." Discern whether there are any patterns between these occurrences. It would be well received if a follow-up question would be asked from a spouse how he or she would like you to prevent that from happening in the future: "How can I prevent you from feeling … rejected, abandoned …?"

Examples of diagnostic or problem-solving questions are the following:

- "Do you feel loved by me?" Since this is a closed-ended question it should be followed up with an open-ended question, for example: "When do you feel loved by me?" or "When do you not feel loved by me?" depending on the first answer received.
- "In which areas can we grow?"
- "If you could change anything about me, what would you change?"
- "Describe what caused you to be most despondent about me?"

It is a good habit to ensure that these conversations end with a positive ending. This can be achieved by asking questions that would leave both of you feeling good. Some of the previous answers might have been painful to hear. Some of the questions might have been painful to answer. When we sit in each other's personal space and see a loved one endure pain it has a very powerful impact on the observer.

When we experience each other's pain it makes us realize what damage we are doing to him or her rather than to realize our own justification for what we have done. It causes us to see what he or she suffers and how that causes him or she to feel, rather than focusing on our own hurt and feelings or reasons to justify what we do. It also motivates us to change. It grants us compassion. In a relationship we are to realize that a person cannot enforce changes he or she wants onto another person. We only have the power and ability to change ourselves. Seeing the pain in a loved one, caused by you, brings about a desire in you to change. It may be tempting to think that it is his or her fault and that you did not affect the hurt and you may be correct. If that is what the other person is convinced of, however, that is the "truth" to him or her. The main thing to remember is to end the discussion positively. The following positive questions could terminate the discussion:

- "What do you like most about me?"
- "You feel most loved when …?"
- "Tell me about it when you are happy with me?"
- "What are your dreams for our relationship?"
- "Tell me a story about one of your best memories about us."

Once this process is complete, switch the roles and the other spouse can now ask the questions. I have led many couples through this process, and I would tell the asking spouse what to ask. At the end of these sessions couples frequently remark the following:

- "We have never had such a deep conversation before."
- "I really feel understood."
- "For the first time I really feel that my spouse has grasped it."
- "I feel a great deal closer to my spouse."
- "Wow, now I feel like we can talk about anything."

The art of talking intimately can transform most relationships. It enriches emotional intimacy, and it bonds couples. It really ignites a fire of closeness and emotional intimacy. We can all learn these skills and invest the time to master the art of talking for surefire emotional intimacy.

❧ CHAPTER TWELVE ❧

USING METAPHORS AS BRIDGES TO UNDERSTANDING

Emotional intimacy is the bonding between people's emotions, thoughts and feelings and it takes place when they are connected to each other. Emotions, thoughts and feelings do not have the ability to leave a spouse's mind magically to connect in mid-air to the partner. Connections are made when a spouse realizes that the partner with whom the communication takes place, experiences or understands the emotions that you are feeling. The same is true when he or she thinks the same thoughts or understands what is thought, or shares the same ideas. When this happens we feel understood, and there is empathy, while feeling united and bonded. This is a wonderful feeling to experience; it feels warmhearted and welcoming, as if there is something special, if not magical, between two people. It draws people even closer together and it creates trust. It creates a desire to want more intimacy.

The depth and privacy of the shared emotions, thoughts, and feelings determines the enormity and significance of the reward gained. To experience the reward even more, couples naturally want to go deeper into each other's hearts and become more private. The depth reached is proportional to the amount of risk involved, as discussed before. It takes risk, but oh! The reward is sweet.

All men and women researched in the doctoral dissertation, and thousands of others who were tested for resonance reported that feeling listened to and understood generate emotional intimacy. Recognizing that a spouse has made the connection and shares the same idea, thoughts, and emotions is what gives us the conviction and feeling of truly being listened to and being understood. Consequently, to connect our inner selves with another creates emotional intimacy; and a great deal of it. Conversely, feeling misunderstood and not listened to leaves us feeling frustrated, empty, alone, and isolated - the very issues that drain emotional intimacy right out of us. Connections made and shared between a person's inner self and a partner are the measure of feeling listened to and understood.

So, how then can we create connections between two peoples' thoughts, and emotions? These senses live within the heart, mind and soul, and cannot be handed out to a loved one. The only way to share them with others and hope that others will feel the same way, or at least understand them, is to share them. We already discussed ways of doing so in chapter ten and eleven. We also discovered that this is more difficult than it sounds. It would be so convenient and satisfying if we could build a bridge from one mind to another so that our exact thoughts, feelings, and emotions could march across that bridge into the other person's mind to be understood the way we intended them. This is not possible, however, and we cannot build such a bridge; but we can come close to this.

Every day teachers use bridges to teach students new ideas, yes, even abstract ideas. They bridge a gap from the known to the unknown. They use an idea with which the students are already familiar and which has some correlation and similarity with the unknown idea. Then they assist the students to start with the familiar idea, and grapple and play with it towards the unknown one; they motivate them to consider and play with similarities and in so doing, to arrive at the unknown. In this way the unknown becomes known, or at least better known through the familiar.

For example, if such a bridge (from the known to the unknown) could not be used, how then could a person explain the concept of beauty to a blind person? Or how would one explain the difference between a pleasant smell and stench to a person who cannot smell? Similarly, how can one explain the difference between melodious orchestral sounds and that of an out of tune garage band to a deaf person?

It is not possible to make the blind person see, smell cannot be restored, and ears cannot be opened. By using bridges from the known to the unknown, however, they can be assisted to at least better understand the concept. In this way the bridge of taste, for example, can be used to bridge the gap of understanding. There are many other bridges that will work just fine too, for example, touch. One could explain something as follows: "You have all tasted food, right? You know how some food tastes good and others not so good. In the same way sight to one's eyes can be pleasant or unpleasant. Smell can be wonderful or awful. Sound can be inspiring or annoying noise." What we have done here is to take a concept that they have all experienced and understood, such as taste, and used the similarity between how taste works to bridge that knowledge towards an unknown concept (like smell, seeing, and hearing). They have not physically seen, smelt or heard, but they could understand the concept. When they enthusiastically reply with: "Oh yeah, I get it," and you see that a new light has gone on in their lives, a connection has been made.

In relationships, a good bridge to use is a metaphor which helps to create understanding and thereby connection. Choosing a metaphor to bridge the gap towards understanding is useful as both parties know and understand the metaphor and can discuss the metaphor as a starting point to move from the known to the unknown. The similarities between the metaphor and the thoughts, ideas, and feelings we wish to communicate form the bridge from the known to the unknown. Metaphors save us a lot of explaining and time. Within minutes metaphors help us to effectively assist someone to feel what we feel or think what we think, or at least it helps us get closer to and more intimate with one another. Metaphors are also easier to discuss than abstract thoughts, which perhaps only one person may have. Both people, however, know something about the metaphor.

Metaphors are also very fluid. Once they help us understand one concept we can play with the metaphor to bring out the next concept. We can also move from one metaphor to the next. Metaphors help us to visualize the situation and they make it easier to place ourselves in the other person's shoes. When we "shared the same shoes", or at least "walked in the same shoes" for a while, even if the "sharing" and "walking" take place in our minds, we are more likely to think and feel the similarly. Even if we do not think and feel the same, at least we would be more inclined to understand our spouse's thoughts and feelings, and why they think and feel their way. When that understanding is reached and our spouses know that we understand better, they would feel understood and emotional intimacy jumps for joy.

Albert's marriage, using a pseudonym as an example, formed part of the research relating to the psychological theories used, even though their marriage was not included in the dissertation. Albert and his wife have been married for a long time. They have been married so long that if they were your parents you would probably tell everyone how long your parents have been married. Unfortunately their marriage is not a happy one. Their relational troubles started very shortly after their wedding. During all the years that they have been married Albert's wife can only think of one short period of eighteen months of bliss. They both agree that they do not have a romantic relationship. They are merely "living together", and their intimate relationship is pretty much dead. The only reason they are still together is because they do not have the resources to separate and, consequently, they are co-dependent.

One day Albert came to my office to see me. He was despondent and having feelings of hopelessness. He was unhappy and she was distressed; both have both been unhappy for longer than many people could even remember. I asked him what the matter was with their relationship. He did not even know where to begin as so much water had flown under their bridge. How could he get me to understand the many things that have been going on for longer than I have been alive? Their relationship is too complex, their history too enormous even to attempt to put it into words. He started an attempt to explain their troubles and then stopped. He started again, this time from a different angle as before. After many attempts to verbalize what has been going on, Albert was visibly frustrated with his inability to put into words that which he had experienced and that which he himself did not understand. Where would he even start?

How could I help Albert to communicate successfully to me and convey just a glimpse of his mind? How could we bridge the understanding gap? Metaphors served us very well that day. Professor Archie Smith, Jr., M.S.W., Ph.D. taught me about using metaphors in this way. He also taught me that there are three entities involved between two people: The first person, the second person and thirdly, their relationship. The relationship between two people develops and *obtains a life of its own.*

During a moment of silence while Albert was thinking how to attempt to tell me what was wrong with their relationship, I took my opportunity and asked the question. "Albert, could you please talk about a metaphor, something else that would appropriately symbolize or represent your relationship?" This was not what Albert expected. He was taken aback, just a little bit. His brain was still tied up in frustration trying to explain his relationship. Now I asked him to think differently, to approach the matter in a different way. It took some explaining on my part to get Albert to understand what I wanted. Once he grasped the idea behind using metaphors as bridges to understanding things snapped into place.

Interestingly, he suddenly did not have to think and the frustration disappeared as he knew instantly what to tell me. Looking sternly straight forward he lifted his straightened hand, as if in a salute, and placed it in front of his nose, between his eyes. As he moved his hand forward away from his face he said, "A cement wall. Our relationship is like a cement wall."

Albert was sure he knew what he discerned about his relationship. I did not know a great deal about their relationship other than that which was public knowledge. In just two short sentences he succeeded in explaining exactly what was going on between him and his wife. These two sentences communicated a great deal more than just their contents. They helped me to understand how Albert felt about his relationship. They told me that he felt that he couldn't "get through" to, or communicate with his wife; the wall was impenetrable. There was separation between them and the separation was solid, entrenched, and build up over a long time. The separation was so severe that one could not even see what was happening on the other side of the wall, as it was not a fence. It also told me that he had very little hope because how could this cement wall be broken down? The similarities between the metaphor (cement wall) and his relationship bridged the gap between the unknown and the known.

I did not know much about their relationship, but I did know something about a cement wall. Using what is known about a cement wall could then be transferred to their relationship. In this way it allowed us to know more about their relationship. He had a hard time verbalizing what was not working in their relationship prior to using the tool, called a metaphor. Even though I did not understand the depth of their struggle I understood the glimpse provided about their relationship with the concept of a cement wall. I understood that cement walls were used to fortify places and that they kept people in or out. Using what is known to me, Albert and I began to talk about the metaphor, and consequently, it moved me from the known, the metaphor, a cement wall, to the unknown, their relationship; then I comprehended their situation and he felt understood.

I wished to know more, however. So, we started to explore the cement wall, but in doing so we were actually exploring the relationship itself. We actually discussed the following questions:

1. "Who built the wall?"
2. "How was the wall built?"
3. "How long did it take to build it?"
4. "Were they still building on the wall or is it completed?"
5. "What was the foundation of the wall?"

These questions provided a lot of insight into what Albert thought and had expired between him and his wife. The first question revealed if Albert was blaming his wife, outsiders, himself, circumstances, or if they both shared some blame. The second question let us know what specifically caused the wall to be built. The third question told us whether their relationship was rocked by a quick major event or damaged over time. I asked the question anyway even though it is common knowledge that cement walls take time to be built and dry out. The next question informed us whether or not damage to their relationship was still continuing. The last question was an attempt to get to the root causes of their troubles.

Albert's facial expressions, his hand motions, and his tone of voice told me that he was feeling hopeless, but I still wished to know how bad he thought the relationship really was; was there hope, even just a glimmer? So I started to play with the metaphor even more; I used the wall metaphor to explore the issue further by asking:

- "Are there any windows in the wall?"

- "Are there any doors in the wall?"
- "Are there any big trees nearby one could climb to see over the wall?"
- "Is the wall sound proof; can audible communication take place?"

Albert was completely relaxed and his frustration disappeared. It seemed as if he enjoyed talking about his relationship with his wife by means of the metaphor. The best of all, however, was that he was able to assist me to understand how he felt. That caused him to feel more understood and he no longer felt so alone. He had someone he could talk to who actually understood, even if just partially. That conversation bonded Albert and me closer together and emotional intimacy was created; we were the best of friends, and just imagine what a conversation like this could achieve to boost emotional intimacy between him and his wife.

When I suggested that he also needs to have a similar conversation with his wife, using metaphors of course, he objected, stating that they could not discuss their relationship without fighting. Like medication, metaphors have side effects too. Luckily the side effect of using metaphors is very positive; discussing a metaphor rather than the relationship directly removes some of the negative emotion involved. With less emotion clouding the discussion, people are generally more balanced, fair, calm, and objective and this was exactly what was needed in situations such as this one. Because metaphors are bridges to understanding and understanding builds emotional intimacy metaphors lead to greater emotional intimacy. Greater emotional intimacy leads to great intimate romantic relationships. Thus, using metaphors are a surefire way to great romantic relationships.

Now that Albert and I discussed his marital relationship, it was time to explore the other two entities involved in the relationship: Albert and his wife. *Sometimes people love each other, but hate their relationship.* Other times people hate each other. If they love each other, but hate their relationship there is hope as the relationship can change and be healed, obviously not in every case, but generally there is more hope. If they hate each other the road ahead presents itself as a steep uphill filled with hazards.

Typically partners are not very good at distinguishing between their feelings towards their relationships and their feelings towards their spouses. People tend to think that what they feel about their relationship is also what they feel towards their spouses. They mistakenly think that the relationship and their spouses are one and the same thing. This kind of reasoning thinks that if the relationship is negative then the spouse is also negative. If a person feels a certain way about the relationship it is assumed that these same feelings are also felt towards a spouse, but this is not always the case. I know many people who suffered in marriage, but the moment they terminated the marital relationship they became good friends. There are many people who love each other but hate the alcoholism that is part of the relationship. Similarly, people may love each other but hate the financial management within the relationship. There are many such examples of where people love each other but have a problem with some part of the relationship.

I had to find out how Albert saw himself and his wife, independently from the relationship.

When I meet people for the first time they often ask me who I am, and I dislike that question. It makes me feel very uncomfortable. What am I supposed to say when someone asks me: "So who is Pierre?" or "What makes Pierre, Pierre?" How do I answer such a question? Most people answer such a question by stating what their professions are, but what one does for a living hardly explains or defines who we are. Many people do not like their jobs. Would it be fair to say that people are what they do even though they do not like what they do? It is easy to ask questions and to answer questions about what a person does, but there is a difference between "knowing about a person" and "knowing a person." We can know so much about a movie star or a sports star without knowing the person. When we are asked who we are we face the same problem Albert struggled with when he first attempted to tell me about their relationship. There is just so much information and per-spectives to share that we do not even know where to begin to answer the question.

So I did not wish to ask Albert directly how he sees his wife and himself. Instead, I used the tool that is a bridge to understanding: The metaphor.

I asked Albert to tell me about a metaphor that would represent him as a person. He broke out in a big smile, his eyes sparkled and his voice was jovial. Without hesitation he said, "I am like a big, quiet, and peaceful river flowing along gently." For the next half-hour we explored his metaphor and it taught me a great deal about Albert and how he regarded himself.

I asked Albert to tell me a metaphor relating to his wife, and we had to realize that his metaphor was looking at his wife from his perspective. We had to be careful that his perspective might or might not necessarily be an accurate reflection of his wife. Once again Albert's demeanor changed; the metaphor he chose to describe his wife consisted of two short words, spoken with certainty and conviction: "A torrent", and this was the power of using metaphors as there were volumes of information embedded in those two short words. We spent a long time talking about "torrents" and the similarity between them and his wife. In the end, I thought I understood pretty well how Albert saw his wife. How could such a complex topic as a person or one's perspective of a person be so well understood while being described by so few words?

Metaphors are extremely powerful and useful as we can take everything we know about the metaphor, which is a great deal more than the description of the metaphor itself, and transfer that knowledge to the person or relationship in question. If a part of the information about the metaphor does not relate accurately to the topic at hand the person who supplied the metaphor can simply correct the inaccuracy by tweaking or modifying the metaphor, or simply making use of a different metaphor. In this manner the conversation can move from one metaphor to another. It is absolutely amazing how much understanding can be gained in such a short time with so few words by using a metaphor as a bridge to understanding; metaphors have a great deal of depth.

Interestingly, Albert's metaphors for him and his wife interact. We explored how one metaphor makes an impact on another, leading us right back to speaking about their relationship once again. Albert mentioned that the torrent makes the peaceful river burst over its banks. He explained how the torrent changes the peaceful river into rushing and dangerous rapids. We saw that the river rapids harm innocent vegetation growing on and near the banks. We discussed whom the vegetation represents.

By the end of our session I understood so much more about Albert and his wife, and their relationship, although it was only from his perspective. Albert felt so much better as there was someone who now also understood him and his situation. He had to express himself and it made sense and we grew closer to each other. Our friendship grew more in that one session than in the previous number of years I have known Albert.

All couples can have the same experience; we can experience super-charged or thrilling emotional intimacy and we can understand more about each other. That understanding can go to deeper depths and become more personal. As that happens, emotional intimacy skyrockets. Please consider using metaphors when you and your spouse enjoy each other's private space relishing the art of talking. How about asking your spouse similar questions to those asked of Albert?

Exploring each other's metaphors is indirectly exploring each other and the relationship. Mutually exploring our relationships bridge the gap of understanding. It lets each other into our secrets (women in particular love this,) into our minds, and into our hearts and emotions. This makes us feel understood. Metaphors are vehicles by which understanding travels from one person to the next thereby enabling us to bridge the gap of understanding. Metaphors become a friendly play dough with which we can play, forming and sculpting what we would like the other person to see, and when this is finished the other person can see and experience something more concrete and tangible than feelings and thoughts. Both spouses can jump in and play until they "get it" or understand and comprehend the situation. Couples really benefit from its use.

Clive and Claire, using them as pseudonymous examples, were getting married within a few months and they came to me for pre-marital counseling. Although they did not meet the research criteria to be included in the doctoral research, I also spent time with them regarding the research as I was curious to observe whether the inclusion criteria would actually make a difference or not. A great deal has been learned from their experience, however, and so I share it here.

Clive and Claire came for pre-marital counseling as they wished to get their marriage off to the best possible start. They still report being very happily married to this day. During one of our sessions together we enjoyed discussing metaphors; I asked Clive and Claire the same three questions posed to Albert:

- "Please describe a metaphor relating to your relationship."
- "Please tell me about a metaphor describing you."
- "Please use a metaphor to describe your fiancé."

Clive said that their relationship was like a beautiful flower garden. This metaphor taught me that he saw their relationship as something beautiful to be enjoyed. It was filled with wonderful fragrances and vibrant colors, meaning that their relationship was exciting and attractive. I asked Clive what his role was in the garden, or perhaps if there was something in the garden representing him. His answer added a new character to the garden metaphor. He saw himself as the gardener who loves caring for the garden. He mentioned that it was his job to ensure that the garden is healthy and beautiful. At times certain plants might need to be pruned at other times they might require water. This metaphor told Claire that Clive was prepared to invest in their relationship and that he would do what was necessary to maintain and develop the garden. It spoke of Clive's willingness to take responsibility for the garden. He saw their relationship as something growing. It revealed that he viewed relationships as something that needed to be worked at to be beautiful.

As long as the garden represented their relationship this metaphor spoke of hope and dreams that their relationship would remain great. If he intended, however, that the garden represent his fiancé instead of their relationship we have a major shift in the interpretation of the metaphor. If this were the case then he was planning to "prune" her to get rid of what he considered to be "dead leaves." He would have seen it as his job to "shape" her. This metaphor resulted in a wonderful discussion between the two of them. Not only did I understand his view of their relationship better, so did his fiancé.

Her metaphor for their relationship was a symphony. At times one instrument would take the lead while the others provide support and background music, and at other times another instrument would take over the melody. She saw their relationship as "give and take" or an equal relationship, as long as there was harmony. One person did not always need to be "in charge." When not in charge the job description was to support the one who is "in charge." Claire viewed their relation-ship as a flowing and fluid masterpiece. At times the music would be loud and exciting and at other times it would be more peaceful and slower. Her view of their relationship is also beautiful and full of hope. They were a team, making the music together.

Since Clive was the gardener in his metaphor I wanted to know from him whom he would like to be in the orchestra, a musician or the conductor? This was an important question as Claire definitely viewed Clive as one of the leading musicians. If Clive wanted to be the conductor it would not have fitted into Claire's picture of their relationship. This would be a serious issue in the relationship. This was also a topic that they had not discussed before. By using metaphors they discovered such a great deal about each other and their relationship. Oh! You must be wondering if Clive thought of himself as the conductor, or not – he did not. They would decide together what piece of music to play and how to play it.

They reported that the metaphor "chat" really provided an easy way to talk about complex topics and that it made it so easy to be "on the same page"; simply to discover what the other person thinks and means. Being "on the same page" with intimate and personal thoughts, feelings, and ideas is what emotional intimacy is all about. They experienced unity in their vision for their relationship, and they felt connected as a couple. They sensed that they understood each other, and emotional intimacy was generated.

Everyone can use metaphors as bridges to understanding on their way to great intimate romantic relationships. Metaphors can also be used during times of conflict. Instead of discussing a highly charged and emotional topic that causes pain, metaphors remove emotion and convey understanding about the issue because metaphors are removed from a person (we are discussing something external like a river or a garden or a cement wall rather than discussing the person directly, yet indirectly and at the same time we are getting at what the issues are). A spouse can say, "Tell me a metaphor about the issue we just faced." A couple can then play with metaphors, explore them and observe their meaning, messages and potential implications.

Metaphors can also be used to explain the way we feel. Asking can easily start conversations: "Tell me a metaphor that explains how you feel right now." Metaphors are a great tool to explore that which is very difficult to explore without their illuminating use.

Whenever we sense that someone is struggling to express or explain themselves it might help to ask them to use a metaphor to express or explain themselves. One significant aspect or key to remember though is not to fall in love with one's own interpretation of the metaphor. We don't want to make the metaphor say what we did not intend to say.

Metaphors should be explored in a safe environment where the interpretation is guided by the one who shared the metaphor in the first place. If the metaphor is misinterpreted the originator can correct us, tweak or fine-tune the metaphor, or simply jump to another metaphor to better explain what the previous metaphor could not explain accurately.

Metaphors are easy to use and fun to play with. In the process of using metaphors we are actually exploring each other and getting to know each other better. Metaphors assist us to get a glimpse of what our spouses feel and think. These intimate connections of understanding create emotional intimacy. Using metaphors is a surefire way to emotional intimacy and as a result creates great intimate romantic relationships.

Pierre F. Steenberg, Ph.D., D.Min.

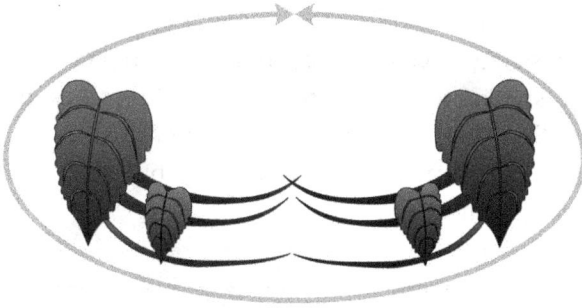

❧ CHAPTER THIRTEEN ❧

PULLING APART – PULLING TOGETHER

All relationships fluctuate naturally; from time to time they swing closer together and from time to time they tend to drift further apart. It is normal to feel closer together at times while feeling further apart during other periods. Levels of emotional intimacy fluctuate all the time. Right after an argument, for example, the level of emotional intimacy is not as high as it may have been prior to the argument. Healthy relationships, however, have a gentle swinging motion, further from and closer to each other. These swings are not always caused by negative events such as arguments; they are simply part of life. People get busy and spend less time together and make it up when the pressure on their lives is reduced. Crises that provide an opportunity of closeness do not happen every day, causing them to count for or earn brownie points. The fact is that a movement from feeling close to feeling further apart and back is a part of the pendulum of emotional intimacy.

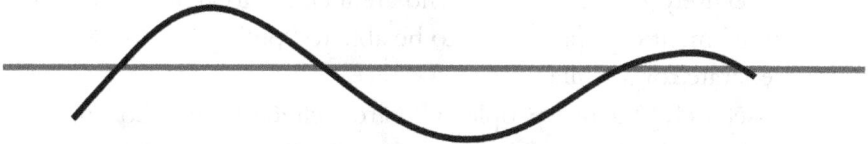

When healthy relationships swing apart they do not swing too far apart. The swinging motion needs to stay within a fairly narrow range. If emotional intimacy swings exceed the narrow range into a broad motion too far apart it indicates serious issues in the relationship. Similarly, these swings need to be on a smooth curve rather than a jagged, uneven shark tooth pattern often seen in stock market charts, because more often than not, shark teeth "bite." It has to be expected that spouses need to be pulling apart at times, but not too far away and in gentle swinging motions.

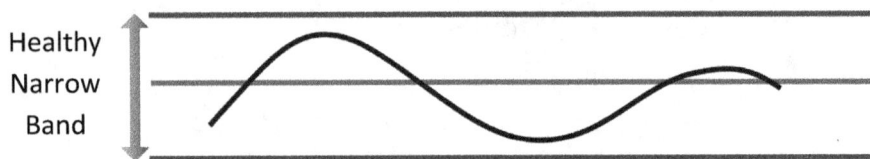

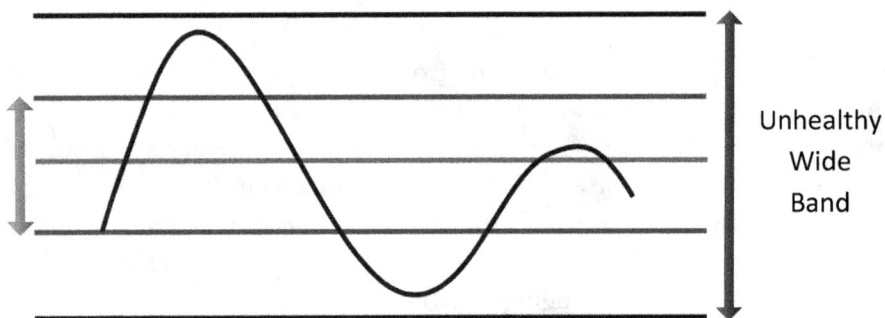

Healthy Narrow Band

Unhealthy Wide Band

When spouses do not "pull apart" in this way, one or both of them tend to feel smothered. They may even fear losing their own identity. Before long a dreaded threat begins to appear in the form of an accusation, "You are too *controlling*":

- Insecurely attached people who are inclined to avoid intense attachment especially need to be able to "pull apart" or be separate for a while.
- Insecurely attached people, who are inclined to be preoccupied with attachment tend not to wish to "pull apart", nor do they want their spouses to "pull apart."

- Securely attached people find the balance between closeness and separation.
- People who are inclined to be introverted need to "pull apart" a bit from time to time and it is more valid for them than it is for extroverted people to want to "pull apart."
- Lastly, men seem to need to "pull apart" more often than women. People merely need a bit of space from time to time.

Since women love to connect they often interpret men's "pulling apart" as rejection or punishment by exclusion. Wives can be tempted to think that their husbands' pulling away means that the husbands are not truly that "into" them as their wives. When a wife comes home after work, more often than not, she wants to bond by sharing what happened during her day. She does this not because she thinks he needs to know what happened, but because sharing these things amounts to the creation of connection and emotional intimacy. When a husband comes home after work, more often than not, he wants to "pull apart" a bit. As connecting "recharges" a women's "batteries", asking a man to give more at home after lots has already been given at work drains his "batteries." The two genders have two different and opposing needs. She desires closeness and bonding while he desires space and time apart when tired, stressed or in need of "recharging" or revitalizing.

This is how the scenario often plays out: The husband and wife get home from work and greet each other briefly on the way in. They each do what needs to be done and then he disappears. She calls him to come and assist with something, not that she needs the help, but because she is yearning for fellowship, bonding and connecting with him. If he answers her call for help he usually says something like, "In a minute," or "Let me just finish this." The proverbial minute and implications of the word "just" however does not result in a quick response. A long time later she calls out again. He hears her, but does not wish to respond. It is not that he does not wish to spend time with her, but he is simply not ready to do that yet. His "batteries" are only halfway "charged" and he would hate to go to her before being fully recharged.

Now, both of them get frustrated. She feels excluded, isolated, and empty, which are female words for being "punished", while he feels nagged, a male word for being "harassed." When he hears her calling him again, he does not make it known to her, but he either rolls his eyes, sighs, or says to himself, "Not again," or "Can I not get some time to myself?" or "What now?" When he is really frustrated he may indulge in all three. During this time of being "separate" they do not relate. When she feels that they do not relate she feels that they do not have a relationship. Her "batteries" are also not being allowed to "recharge" in his absence, and she is not being recharged because interaction and connecting charges her "batteries."

His presence and relating to her is her invigorator or "charger." Her absence and not dealing with anything is what refills him with energy. Usually husbands will be spacing out or position them in front of a computer, television, etc. If this is the case, how can the husband and wife both be refilled with energy at the same time? If they cannot be invigorated simultaneously, who gets the opportunity to be invigorated first? Logic demands that the most worn out "battery" is to be "charged" firstly. This is no easy solution, however, as we do not have "battery level indicators." Human experience involving more than one person cannot be measured, quantified and compared objectively. There is no way to determine whose energy levels is the lowest, unless it is really obvious as in the case of illness.

The first thing to realize is to understand each other's needs. We tend to interpret our loved one's actions through the lens of our own gender, from comprehending ourselves in the first place as a point of departure. This leads to misinterpretation, which in turn misfires or smothers emotional intimacy. She understands that she is invigorated through bonding and sharing, therefore, she also thinks mistakenly that he is refilled with energy in the same way. So, when he walks into their home talking about how tired he is she gladly assumes that he wishes to be recharged by bonding and sharing with her, because that is what works for her.

Her interpretation creates an expectation in her mind as that is exactly what she desires to happen to her to be refilled with energy. What could be better for a tired woman than to sit with her husband and bond, creating a connection, and getting closer together at the same time? Then when he disappears, "favoring" the computer to her, her expectation is shattered. Now she thinks that when her husband prefers to sit in front of a screen rather than to bond and connect with her there must be something wrong and that she is being "ignored" at best or "punished" at worst. This thinking, however, is based on how women think and operate, not men.

Similarly, he hears her saying how tired she is when they meet, and he thinks, "Great, tonight will not be demanding, we both will merely space out and relax until we are done recharging." An expectation is created in his mind based on his male understanding of reinvigoration; when she calls him his expectation is shattered. He interprets the situation by way of his understanding, which is wrong as she does not think and operate as he does. His misinterpretation labels her as demanding. He feels that she is in the way of his desire of being refilled with energy.

If we understood each other's needs and thinking, however, it would change our interpretation of the situation. As our interpretations are mostly negative when it comes to these kinds of situations, it is important to think from the other person's point of view. These type of situations need to be interpreted differently, from the point of view of the spouse. That does not change the fact that "batteries are running low" and are in need of "recharging." Neither does it change the different ways in which women's and men's "batteries recharge." Understanding the different needs and interpretations of men and women should end negative interpretations of the other spouse and produces acceptance and sympathy, resulting in accommodation of the partner.

Whether men understand it or not, women need to spend time with their partner to bond and connect. There is certainly a time for women to go shopping together, for example, to be able to be invigorated by her friends. If refilling of energy only took place with other women, however, husbands should not be surprised if women shared more emotional intimacy with other women than with them as their husbands. Wives wish to connect, bond and seek emotional intimacy with their husbands as well. A woman's call is often not a call for him to do something, but for bonding time. She is not demanding, however, she is simply in desperate need for companionship and emotional intimacy; it is a cry for some time together.

Whether women understand it or not, men need some time apart; there is no magical way to accelerate his "recharging" process to take less time. When he wishes to be alone it is neither because anything is wrong, nor is anyone being "punished." It does not mean that he does not wish to spend time with her; it merely means that he is drained and not ready to do so at that moment. When in doubt, ask him or her. If she feels that he is "punishing" her, she could *simply ask* him in a non-judgmental and non-demanding way whether that is true or not. If he is convinced that she was nagging him and was demanding, he could just ask her in an accepting and loving way whether that was the case or not.

A person's comprehension derived from an interpretation of the other person's position is only valid if it is done from the other person's perspective. One cannot accurately "decode" another's behavior or sometimes even words, using the interpreter's own mindset. The minds of men and women simply do not "operate" in the same way. It is when "the way we work" stands in opposition to, or in the way of each other that emotional intimacy is diminished.

When a husband is "forced" to spend time with his wife when he is not ready to, it does not really reinvigorate either of them. It does not "charge" her "battery" if he spends time with her as a result of being "forced" into it. For women, emotional intimacy can only grow if he spends time with her because he really wants to. It does not charge his "battery" either, as he has to withdraw and space out for his "battery" to recharge. When a wife is "forced" to forego fellowship with her husband in the name of his "recharging" time, she feels empty and punished. No one wins and both of them loose out.

There has to be a way to solve this dilemma for emotional intimacy and closeness to grow. A way has to be found to cease the negative effect one's "recharging" has on the other, and vice versa. As long as his need for spacing out was preventing her need to bond and to be fulfilled, she would pay a huge price. As long as her need for bonding stands in the way of his need to space out, he would keep on labeling her negatively. He just wishes to be alone, without any strings attached. She just wishes to be together. Without being together she may feel torn apart. If he feels that he is being "forced" into companionship it further drains his "battery." Consequently, meaningful emotional intimacy demands mutual understanding.

From his perspective the solution is simply, "Just leave me alone." From her perspective the solution is simply, "Let's just bond." The problem is that you cannot experience both at the same time. If he gets home from work before she does, he can relax and space out, and hopefully be "charged up" before she gets home. If she gets home after work before he does, his problem, however, gets even worse. By the time he gets home she is done with what she needed to do. She is done bonding with the kitchen; now she is ready to bond with him without him having at least the time she would have been in the kitchen had they arrived home at the same time. Traditional gender roles within typical marriages are assumed here (although that may not always be the case). If this is not the case with your marriage, as more and more marriages work differently, please apply these approaches or "principles" to your particular case.

Wives wish their husbands to understand how unloved, isolated, left out, punished, robbed of emotional intimacy and being left alone they really feel when their husbands leave them alone to be busy with "non-essentials" such as spacing out, rather than to be with them to bond. The longer men "pull apart" the more "torn apart" women feel. Feeling disconnected from her husband tears apart the wife's emotional intimacy. It would be exceedingly helpful if he could find a way to limit his time of spacing out. There is no real reason to be inattentive and absent-minded all evening. Surely, whatever is done during relaxation time is less important than neglecting her, resulting in the relationship pulling further and further apart.

Relaxation or spacing out is important and needed. It would greatly help for her to understand his need for relaxing on his own, and perhaps they could agree on a limited time for his relaxing and spacing out. It is important for him to stick to this agreement and not to exceed the allotted time.

When the allotted time is over they can "pull together" again. A woman feels that when she does not experience her husband's presence, she does not *have* him, she does not experience love and she lacks fulfillment.

Husbands need their wives to understand fully how nagging and making demands on them suck the life out of them. Men need their wives' consent to simply be, or be on their own – without being disturbed for a short time to recharge. She believes that it is worthwhile for both of them to be together when they get home tired after work, but her nagging causes him to label her as "high maintenance." Having what he thinks is a "high maintenance" wife requires more energy to deal with, when what he needs is to recharge his "batteries" not expel more energy from them. "Holding a gun to his head" and telling him to love her would not be genuine love, and it is certainly not a valid way to convince him to be emotionally intimate. Using the art of talking can be a great deal more beneficial to work out how the different needs are to be accommodated. As about everything in life, emotional intimacy can be developed by doing certain things, as indicated previously, and by avoiding others. The battle between "pulling apart" and "pulling together" is one of the things to be avoided by working it out before it damages emotional intimacy seriously.

The facts are, she needs bonding and he needs spacing out or relaxing. To fulfill her need he can help by seeing to it that he does not relax too long and, importantly after that, spending quality time with her to bond; or, alternatively, they can connect first and then leave time for him to space out. To fulfill his need she can provide him with pre-determined relaxation time, and make sure to leave him alone during that time.

Great intimate romantic relationships naturally "pull apart" and "pull together" again. The narrower this range of movement is kept, the greater emotional intimacy ensues. Working together to create gentle "pulling apart" and "pulling together" emotions help to achieve this goal on the way to surefire fulfilling romantic relationship.

❧ CHAPTER FOURTEEN ❧

EMOTIONAL INTIMACY AS CHOICE

People are interpretive by nature. We interpret everything. We interpret what is said and not said, body language, what happens with us and around us. We even interpret what we think should have happened, but did not. We also attempt to interpret abstract and non-accessible features such as people's motives and thoughts. We interpret because we simply have to make sense of things, and interpretation is an attempt to clarify what we perceive. Sometimes we are very perceptive and make accurate interpretations. At other times our interpretations can be way off. Unless we make our analyses known and ask whether or not they are accurate we tend to automatically think that our interpretations are correct. Our interpretations, however, are often dead wrong.

Martha and Caitlyn, had a professional relationship through Martha's occupation. As a result they interacted with each other on a regular basis. One day Martha interpreted one of Caitlyn's actions as indicative of the "fact" that Caitlyn hated her. A while later Martha mustered all her courage to confront Caitlyn about her "hatred" as she assumed that her interpretation was correct; after all it seemed very clear that Caitlyn hated her. So, instead of asking Caitlyn whether she hated her or not, Martha asked her why she hated her. Caitlyn was taken by total surprise for she did not hate Martha at all, in fact, Caitlyn considered Martha to be a good friend. Caitlyn and Martha are good friends to this day.

When I heard about the "confrontation" I approached Martha and asked her what caused her to think that Caitlyn "hated" her? Without hesitation Martha recalled what Caitlyn did. My next question resulted in a long silence with no answer, causing Martha to reconsider the whole situation. I asked Martha, "Could there be any other possible reasons, apart from "hatred", why Caitlyn did what she did that would explain her actions equally well"? Brainstorming together Martha and I came up with a number of alternative reasons that would also have made perfect sense of Caitlyn's actions. None of these alternative reasons had anything to do with destructive feelings towards Martha.

I was still curious; if there were numerous possible explanations for Caitlyn's actions, why did Martha pick the interpretation of "hatred"? So I asked Martha, and I expected her to say that perhaps there was some negative history with bad feelings between her and Caitlyn that favored this interpretation; perhaps some destructive comments were made between them. To my surprise Martha did not report any negativity between them prior to this event; in fact, Martha recalled that she never even thought of any other possible explanations of Caitlyn's actions. What made her so certain that Caitlyn "hated" her was a remark from a third party. This remark coupled with Caitlyn's actions seemed to make sense; consequently, Martha accepted the conclusion that Caitlyn "hated" her as fact.

I could not wait to speak to Caitlyn. Caitlyn confirmed that the motive behind her actions was nothing personal against Martha; she had no problem with Martha, and they were good friends.

How then did the third party wrongly conclude that Caitlyn "hated" Martha? I then asked Caitlyn what she said to this third person. She reported that nothing said between her and this person had anything to do with adverse feelings towards Martha. The third person, however, interpreted Caitlyn's action as "hatred" towards Martha and we did not know why this wrong interpretation was made. The person then told Martha that Caitlyn "hated" her as if it were a fact. The certainty with which Martha had been told that Caitlyn "hated" her convinced her that it must be true.

Relationships can very quickly become complicated. A person's incorrect interpretation influenced another person's interpretation; because these two people now interpret the situation in the same way they assume that it must be true, right? In this case it turned out to be totally false. None of these parties would have known the truth if Martha did not ask Caitlyn herself. If Martha did not ask Caitlyn about this invalid interpretation its conclusion would have had a negative impact on their future relationship. It would have become part of their history. This false interpretation would then have been consulted during future interpretations and in this way it would have influenced all future interpretations. As a result these future interpretations might have been incorrect too. Their future relationship would have probably gotten worse and worse simply because of a single person's incorrect interpretation which was shared with Martha.

As we have discovered, we often accept our interpretation of interactions with people as a "fact." At times those interpretations are totally wrong, and at other times they are spot on. Often these interpretations are partially correct and to some extent wrong. As long as we cling to our interpretations as objective truth they will influence us as though they were actually true. Many friendships have been ruined because of assumed interpretations. These relationships do not have to be wrecked as that which destroys them is incorrect and invalid interpretations in the first place.

It was a few minutes before 9:30 one morning. I was ready to walk on stage to address a waiting audience of a specific organization. One of the leaders of the organization walked in behind the stage and tapped me on the shoulder: "There is someone at the side door wishing to speak to you," he said, pointing to the relevant door. I looked up to see who wished to speak to me at such an inopportune time. There was only a minute or two left before the beginning of my speech. The audience was already waiting, and how could I speak to someone right now? At the door stood a scruffy-looking man I never saw before. His hair has obviously not been groomed recently as it stood up in all directions. His clothes were wrinkled and dirty. He looked restless, and he turned around all the time and looked around him in similar fashion as his hair stood up. I wondered whether he might be running away from somebody. The leader of the organization spoke again and said, "His eyes were red." I had to take a decision: Should I let the audience wait and speak to this man, or should I let the man wait and speak to the audience first?

During the few moments of indecision I recalled numerous times when homeless people, like this one, for example, lied to me, dropped the food I had given them on the ground, since they did not receive money instead, and how demanding and angry many became when I did not have the right amount of money available to pacify their desires. Please, I do not wish to be misinterpreted in such a way as to construe that these comments mean that I dislike homeless people; nor do all homeless people behave in this way. I have unquestionably assisted hundreds of homeless people prior to this one; yes, hundreds. As I weighed up what to do I heard the cue from the hall inviting me to walk on stage to address the crowd. My decision was easy; this man could wait, he is in the minority and all these other people also need my attention now, they too were waiting for me. I asked the leader of the organization to apologize politely to the homeless man and to explain to him that I had to speak to the audience immediately, but that he was very welcome to meet me after the meeting. I pledged to make time for him directly after my appointment.

When I had finished my speech and after all the formalities I went looking for the homeless man, but he was nowhere to be found. I asked around whether someone had seen him and eventually someone told me that he had spoken to this man; he disclosed the surprising story of this person:

The supposedly homeless man was not homeless at all and his "red eyes" were not due to alcohol. The previous night his teenage son with a few friends in the car was driving home on a notoriously dan-gerous road and there was an accident; one of his son's friends was killed and some of the others were injured. The police charged this son with reckless driving (he was sober), as if all this was not enough. The father did not sleep all night and his clothing was dirty as he was dealing with the wreckage; his eyes were red because he cried a great deal. He was in pain and tried to speak to me for help.

What did I do? I sent someone away in need and catered to those whose need was pale in comparison. I caused further hurt to a brokenhearted person and I shunned someone who was reaching out for help at a time of his deepest distress. I interpreted the situation wrongly. In the process I shattered any emotional intimacy we could have had and triggered more destructive emotion so intense that I did not know whether this man would ever forgive me. The severe crisis presented an

144

opportunity for abundant emotional intimacy, but I failed the person that day and possibly irreparably damaged all future emotional intimacy between us.

How many relationships have suffered the same catastrophe simply because a situation was misinterpreted? Undoubtedly, all the clues were there to suggest that my interpretation, which I followed, was correct, as not many people would show up at that kind of meeting looking like that. He certainly appeared as a homeless person. If indeed he was a homeless person he had nothing to do all day and all day to do it in. What was another hour for him as my audience was waiting; surely he could have waited?

We are often convinced that our interpretation is correct as we have observed all the clues, and the evidence seems to support our conclusions. Yet, with hindsight it would have been so easy merely to ask the man about the purpose of his visit. Whenever we make an important interpretation we may just as well ask whether or not our conclusions are correct. This little step can act as a huge shield to protect emotional intimacy, and, what is more, scrutinizing our interpretations can prevent a great deal of damage to our relationships.

All people always interpret interactions, Period. These interpretations are based on the contexts of communication and interaction; we interpret what is disclosed and even what is not said. We include what we observe (body language and related clues), similar prior interactions with people, as well as our own context, (like how we feel at that time) into our interpretation. Interpretation is a complicated business. Some people are better equipped to make more balanced interpretations than others. People who are generally well equipped for more accurate interpretation are said to be "objective", while those who are typically not so suited for more accurate interpretation are said to be "subjective."

If objectivity was placed at one end of a spectrum and subjectivity at the other, indicating two extremes, we can chart people on this continuum. Most people, however, are more objective than subjective. The most beneficial place to be on this continuum, however, is not in the middle, but rather closer to the objective end as indicated by the smaller left side of the arrow below. People who fall in the section indicated by the left arched arrow are in the majority and it is definitely the better place find one self. People who fall in the section indicated by the right arched arrow are more prone to jump to wrong conclusions, and it is very difficult to persuade them of other points of view as they find it more difficult to place themselves in other people's shoes. Jumping to unwarranted conclusions has never been considered to be good exercise.

The right arched arrow ends quite a distance away from the end of the spectrum. The left arched arrow also stops short of the end of the spectrum, but less so. People who are on either side of the arched arrows find themselves at the ends of the spectrum; this is not the best place to be at. The most problematic place to be in is far more to the subjective side at the end of the spectrum; in fact, this area presents serious challenges to those who live here.

This is a dangerous place from where to approach life as excessive subjectivity can actually become delusion. People can become so subjective that they only live according to the interpretations of their own minds, which may be devoid of any reality. They live in a world which they create in their minds; a world which is nowhere close to reality. In severe cases "voices" may be heard which do not really exist. Where we are on this line makes a vast direct impact on our relationships and on our emotional intimacy. The accuracy of our interpretations are influenced by our position on the continuum. Our open-mindedness to other possible interpretations is also influenced by our placement on the continuum. The extent to which we cling to our interpretations is yet again influenced by our position on the continuum. Even the time it takes to interpret relational interaction is influenced by our position on this scale.

Objective people take a long time and consider more options before coming to a conclusion and decision. Subjective people tend to make interpretations more quickly and take less information into account when interpreting. Objective people are more willing to reconsider multiple interpretations. For more information on objectivity versus subjectivity and the assessment thereof, please consult someone registered and certified to administer the Taylor Johnson Temperament Analysis material or a similar assessment.

It may be useful to get into the habit of "thinking twice" before we fall in love with any interpretation. There is a great deal to be gained by considering other possible interpretations. Most importantly, however, is that we can check with a spouse whether or not our interpretation is correct or not.

What if we could choose the best possible interpretation for the relationship, provided this interpretation is sensible? Positive subjective interpretations are acceptable to a certain extent. Negative interpretations require more objectivity. What if we saw emotional intimacy as a choice? What if we intentionally choose emotional intimacy, when possible? It is a powerful thought to think that we can choose emotional intimacy by choice. Let's look at an example.

Their financial situation is tight and money is scarce. One day she works late and, consequently, he has various choices of interpretation. He could interpret her working late as follows:

- "She works late as she does not wish to be with me."
- "She works late as she likes being with her co-workers more than with me."
- "She works late as she loves me, she knows our finances are tight and she is doing her best to assist us."
- "She works late because she needs to meet a deadline for her work."

The first two interpretations are negative. The third interpretation is positive. The last interpretation is a neutral one as far as emotional intimacy is concerned.

These examples indicate how the interpretation of her working late influences their emotional intimacy. They also indicate how different interpretations are possible in the same situation. What a shame that we often choose an interpretation or explanation that damages our emotional intimacy, without justification for such interpretation. There was no information to substantiate the negative interpretations in this case. Many, however, choose destructive interpretations void of any supportive information. There are even those who choose a negative interpretation in the face of information indicating a positive interpretation. In many cases we choose an undesirable interpretation of something that can go either way; if that is the case based on the information at hand, would it not make more sense then, to choose the constructive interpretation?

Destructive interpretations have a negative effect on our emotional intimacy. They tend to set in motion a set of consequences that reflect negatively on our spouses' behavior and motifs, and if allowed to continue, end up breaking down our spouse's characters. If positive interpretations are chosen they build up spouses rather than harm the relationship and emotional intimacy.

Emotional intimacy can be a real choice; when negative "evidence" presents itself begging to be interpreted destructively it makes more sense to be as objective as possible. "Objectivity" implies that we attempt to exclude feelings and emotions from the interpretation and instead we examine the facts. Of course there may be reasons for being upset, but the feeling of being upset does not necessarily have a bearing on the interpretation itself. We will be better off by examining all the possible explanations and interpretations. What about this novel idea "ask for more information" before we interpret, should more information be required?

When neutral information presents itself for interpretation why not chose a positive interpretation that stimulates emotional intimacy? When positive information comes to light it would be beneficial to take hold of it, cherish it, and to use it to develop more emotional intimacy. After all, our partner is our spouse and we are on the same side.

Many people come to talk to me as they battle with emotional intimacy as a choice. Effectively their spouses do nothing wrong, but they think that their spouses are the "villains" who escaped from yesterday's "horror movie." No one seems to agree with them, but that does not raise a red flag to them, raising the question of a destructive interpretation. It does not seem to matter that everyone else loves and trusts our spouses. If a "final" decision would be made, they would cling to it more passionately and more strongly than to the spouse in question. Even if he were to bring home a beautiful bush of roses, she would still interpret his gift as intending "to make her sneeze." Even if he told her that he loved her she would still interpret his words of love as an accusation of her. Her reasoning may follow the following course: "The only reason why you say you love me is because, by doing that, you intend to accuse me of not loving you. You are actually saying that you love me, but that I do not love you back." When someone's subjectivity becomes so intense that they live within a world devoid of reality created in their own minds, they need to be advised to seek professional medical attention. Most people though can be shown and be convinced that many of their interpretations are simply based on their choices; that choice is very powerful - it can either "power up" and stimulate emotional intimacy or it can "power down" and ruin emotional intimacy.

It is especially enlightening for us to see emotional intimacy as a choice. We do not realize it, but we often choose the interpretation we have decided upon, despite the fact that more positive interpretations were equally possible or even desirable.

The time has come to face our intimacy issues and it is vital for us to regard emotional intimacy as a choice. We have the power to choose positive interpretations when neutral interactions are observed. We have an obligation to dig deep into the well of objectivity before we choose to swallow negative emotional intimacy when negative inter-pretations seem more logical. A relationship worth having demands that we have to ask our spouses for their side of the story before we lock "finally" into any interpretation, especially when we have no other choice but to choose a negative interpretation as the evidence in its favor seems overwhelming. When it comes to situations that can be interpreted in multiple ways we can choose the positive interpretation. In situations such as these:

- I choose to believe that my spouse loves me.
- I choose to believe that she does everything she can to benefit my welfare.
- I choose to believe that if she did something that could not be interpreted in any other way but destructively, she would have had a very good reason that would explain it in a more positive light.

- I choose to refrain from any harmful interpretation until I understand her (possible positive) explanation.
- I choose to see her positively.
- I choose to see us as partners, both working hard to build up emotional intimacy.
- I refuse to choose damaging interpretations unless she clearly confirms it.
- I CHOOSE SUREFIRE EMOTIONAL INTIMACY!

Emotional intimacy can be a choice. If at all possible we could look at everything our spouses do as something they did because he or she loves us. This point of view looks at him or her and sees love. This choice will grow emotional intimacy greatly. When pondering about whether, "He or she loves me", or "He or she loves me not", and swaying between, "Loves me, loves me not," I will choose "love" over "loves me not" any time. *If we see our spouses as love and loving, we would love them even more.* If we read into what our spouses did as wonderful positive emotional intimacy rather than negative "love me not" behavior, emotional intimacy becomes the beneficiary and our relationships will flourish.

Viewing emotional intimacy as a choice places cupid's arrows in our quivers, the very sight of which drives relational breakdown away. Interpreting what he or she does negatively without a justified cause is like pricking a hole in the balloon of emotional intimacy just because a pin happens to be among the other items on the table. It is better to lean towards the objective side of the continuum when confronted with what looks like negative evidence. It is better to slightly lean towards the subjective side of the continuum when evidence suggests something positive about your spouse.

Imagine you see your spouse walking into a hotel with someone from the opposite sex during his or her lunch break. Negative subjectivity suggests that he or she is having an affair. Objectivity suggests that he or she has never provided any reason to indicate unfaithfulness hence there must be another explanation. That night you ask your spouse about his or her lunch hour. He or she replies that it was an uneventful lunch. You also begin to notice that your spouse is on the phone a lot more than usual. When you move in closer he or she stops speaking on the phone or changes topics. You can see that your spouse is attempting to hide something from you. What if you saw him or her a second time at the same hotel with the same person as before? How would you interpret this situation?

Three weeks later a friend of yours invites you to have dinner to discuss some business and he or she takes you to a restaurant situated in that hotel. As you walk in all your friends come out of hiding; it is a surprise birthday party for you that your spouse arranged!

It is really easy to choose the negative interpretation. It is quite often the wrong interpretation. We owe it to our spouses to be more careful with how we interpret life. It is important to realize that our interpretations are not the truth; they are only interpretations. When events seem negative it is best to ask our spouses what is really going on before we jump to conclusions. Without making ourselves gullible and making it easy for others to take us for a "ride" we can choose the positive interpretations over the negative ones.

What is your choice? For surefire emotional intimacy I choose to interpret what my wife does as positive whenever possible.

✑ THE END ✑

ABOUT THE AUTHOR

Pierre F. Steenberg attained a B.A. Theology degree from Andrews University, Michigan. He also accomplished a B.A. Honors in Biblical Studies, an M.A. in Biblical Studies and a Ph.D. in New Testament Studies from the University of Pretoria in South Africa. Both the M.A. and the Ph.D. were attained with distinction - the highest possible grade presented at a South African University. He graduated more recently *Magna Cum Laude* with a D.Min. in Pastoral Psychology and Family Therapy from the Pacific School of Religion, Berkeley, California. He is a member of numerous academic societies in both theology and counseling, including the Society of Biblical Literature and the American Association of Christian Counselors. He is the author of a number of articles and books.

Pierre has been a pastor and a counselor for many years, enjoying the credentials of the BCCC (Board Certified Christian Counselor) from the International Board of Christian Counselors. He is married to Karlien and they have two sons. The Steenberg family lives in California. Pierre enjoys photography and travel.

Also available from the author (available at Amazon.com and other retailers):

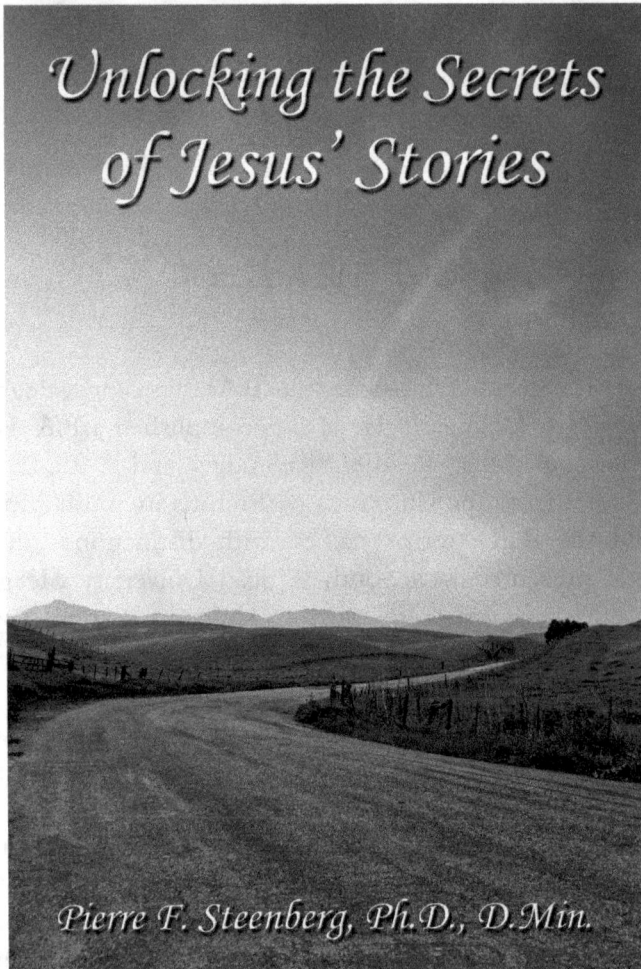

Coming soon:

Relational Safety 101: The Surefire Way to Secure Romantic Relationships

Relational Commitment 101: The Surefire Way to Lasting Romantic Relationships

Physical Intimacy 101: The Surefire Way to Satisfying Romantic Relationships

www.ingramcontent.com/pod-product-compliance
Lightning Source LLC
Chambersburg PA
CBHW060901280326
41934CB00007B/1142